HOLIDAY
COOKIES

COOKIES & TREATS TO MAKE WITH THE FAMILY

pil

Publications International, Ltd.

Microwave Cooking: Microwave ovens vary in wattage. Use the cooking times as guidelines and check for doneness before adding more time.

TABLE OF
CONTENTS

HOLIDAY
ESSENTIALS

CHOCOLATE CHIP COOKIES

MAKES ABOUT 16 COOKIES

2 cups all-purpose flour

1 teaspoon baking soda

½ teaspoon salt

¾ cup (1½ sticks) butter, softened

¾ cup packed brown sugar

½ cup granulated sugar

1 egg

1¼ teaspoons vanilla

8 ounces bittersweet chocolate, chopped, or chocolate chips

Flaky sea salt (optional)

1 Whisk flour, baking soda and ½ teaspoon salt in medium bowl.

2 Beat butter and sugars in large bowl with electric mixer on medium-high speed until light and fluffy. Add egg and vanilla; beat until blended. Add flour mixture; beat on low speed until blended. Stir in chocolate. For best flavor and texture, refrigerate up to 2 days, or dough can be baked immediately.

3 Preheat oven to 350°F. Line cookie sheets with parchment paper. For each cookie, shape about 2 tablespoons of dough into a ball; place on prepared cookie sheets. Sprinkle with sea salt, if desired.

4 Bake about 12 minutes or until edges are lightly browned. Cool cookies on cookie sheets 5 minutes. Remove to wire racks; cool completely.

BUTTERY ALMOND CUTOUTS

MAKES ABOUT 3 DOZEN COOKIES

1½ cups granulated sugar

1 cup (2 sticks) butter, softened

¾ cup sour cream

2 eggs

3 teaspoons almond extract, divided

1 teaspoon vanilla

1 teaspoon baking powder

1 teaspoon baking soda

½ teaspoon salt

4⅓ cups all-purpose flour

2 cups powdered sugar

2 tablespoons milk

1 tablespoon light corn syrup

Assorted food coloring, decorating gels, decorating sugars, sprinkles and decors

1 Beat granulated sugar and butter in large bowl with electric mixer on medium speed until light and fluffy. Add sour cream, eggs, 2 teaspoons almond extract, vanilla, baking powder, baking soda and salt; beat until smooth. Gradually add flour on low speed until blended. Divide dough into four pieces; shape each piece into a disc. Wrap each disc tightly with plastic wrap. Refrigerate at least 3 hours or up to 3 days.

2 Combine powdered sugar, milk, corn syrup and remaining 1 teaspoon almond extract in small bowl; stir until smooth. Cover and refrigerate until ready to use or up to 3 days.

3 Preheat oven to 375°F. Working with one disc of dough at a time, roll out on floured surface to ¼-inch thickness. Cut out shapes using 2½-inch cookie cutters. Place cutouts 2 inches apart on ungreased cookie sheets. Bake 7 to 8 minutes or until edges are set and lightly browned. Remove to wire racks; cool completely.

4 Divide powdered sugar mixture among three or four small bowls; tint each with desired food coloring. Frost and decorate cookies as desired; let stand until set.

NOTE: To freeze dough, place wrapped discs in resealable plastic food storage bags. Thaw at room temperature before using. Or cut out dough, bake and cool cookies completely. Freeze unglazed cookies for up to 2 months. Thaw and glaze as desired.

BLACK AND WHITE COOKIES

MAKES 18 COOKIES

COOKIES

- 2 cups all-purpose flour
- 1 tablespoon cornstarch
- ¾ teaspoon baking soda
- ½ teaspoon salt
- ¾ cup (1½ sticks) butter, softened
- 1 cup granulated sugar
- 2 eggs
- 1 teaspoon vanilla
- ½ teaspoon grated lemon peel
- ⅔ cup buttermilk

ICINGS

- 3½ cups powdered sugar, divided
- 3 tablespoons plus 3 teaspoons boiling water, divided
- 1 tablespoon lemon juice
- 2 teaspoons corn syrup, divided
- ¼ teaspoon vanilla
- 3 ounces unsweetened chocolate, melted

1 Preheat oven to 350°F. Line cookie sheets with parchment paper.

2 Whisk flour, cornstarch, baking soda and salt in small bowl.

3 Beat butter and granulated sugar in large bowl with electric mixer on medium-high speed until light and fluffy. Beat in eggs, one at a time; beat in 1 teaspoon vanilla and lemon peel. Add flour mixture alternately with buttermilk, beating on low speed until blended after each addition. Scrape bowl with rubber spatula and stir a few times to bring the dough together. Using dampened hands, shape 3 tablespoons of dough into a ball for each cookie. Place on prepared cookie sheets 3 inches apart.

4 Bake 13 to 15 minutes or until tops are puffed and edges are lightly browned. Cool on cookie sheets 1 minute. Remove to wire racks; trim any crispy browned edges, if desired. Cool completely.

5 Place 2 cups powdered sugar in small bowl; whisk in 1 tablespoon boiling water, lemon juice and 1 teaspoon corn syrup until smooth and well blended. If necessary, add additional 1 teaspoon water to make smooth, thick and spreadable icing. Spread over half of each cookie; place on wire rack or waxed paper. Place remaining 1½ cups powdered sugar in another small bowl; whisk in 2 tablespoons boiling water, remaining 1 teaspoon corn syrup and ¼ teaspoon vanilla. Whisk in chocolate until smooth and well

blended. If necessary, add additional 1 to 2 teaspoons boiling water to make smooth, thick and spreadable icing. If icing seizes, continue whisking in hot water until it comes back together. Spread icing on other side of each cookie. Place on wire rack; let stand until set. Cookies are best the day they're made, but they can be stored in airtight container at room temperature for 1 to 2 days.

PECAN FLORENTINES

MAKES ABOUT 3 DOZEN COOKIES

¾ cup pecan halves, finely ground*

½ cup all-purpose flour

⅓ cup packed brown sugar

¼ cup light corn syrup

¼ cup (½ stick) butter

2 tablespoons milk

⅓ cup semisweet chocolate chips

*To grind pecans, place in food processor or blender. Process until thoroughly ground with a dry, not pasty, texture.

1 Preheat oven to 350°F. Line cookie sheets with foil; lightly grease foil.

2 Combine pecans and flour in small bowl. Combine brown sugar, corn syrup, butter and milk in medium saucepan. Bring to a boil over medium heat, stirring constantly. Remove from heat; stir in flour mixture.

3 Drop by teaspoonfuls about 3 inches apart onto prepared cookie sheets. Bake 10 to 12 minutes or until lacy and golden brown. (Cookies are soft when hot, but become crisp as they cool.) Cool completely on foil. Slide cookies on foil onto counter or wire racks.

4 Melt chocolate chips. Place in small resealable food storage bag; cut off small corner of bag. Squeeze chocolate decoratively over cookies. Peel cookies off foil.

DANISH RASPBERRY RIBBONS

MAKES ABOUT 6 DOZEN COOKIES

1 cup (2 sticks) butter, softened

½ cup granulated sugar

1 egg

2 tablespoons milk

2 teaspoons vanilla

¼ teaspoon almond extract

2⅔ cups all-purpose flour

6 tablespoons seedless raspberry jam

GLAZE

½ cup powdered sugar

1 tablespoon milk

1 teaspoon vanilla

1 Beat butter and granulated sugar in large bowl with electric mixer on medium speed until light and fluffy. Beat in egg, 2 tablespoons milk, 2 teaspoons vanilla and almond extract until well blended.

2 Gradually add 1½ cups flour, beating on low speed until well blended. Stir in enough remaining flour with spoon to form stiff dough. Shape dough into disc. Wrap in plastic wrap; refrigerate until firm, at least 30 minutes or overnight.

3 Preheat oven to 375°F. Divide dough into six equal pieces. With floured hands, shape one piece at a time into ¾-inch-thick rope, about 12 inches long. (Keep remaining dough pieces wrapped in refrigerator.) Place ropes 2 inches apart on ungreased cookie sheets. Make ¼-inch-deep groove down center of each rope with handle of wooden spoon or finger.

4 Bake 12 minutes. (Ropes will flatten to ½-inch-thick bars.) Remove from oven; spoon 1 tablespoon jam into each groove. Return to oven; bake 5 to 7 minutes or until bars are light golden brown. Cool on cookie sheets 15 minutes.

5 For glaze, whisk powdered sugar, 1 tablespoon milk and 1 teaspoon vanilla in small bowl until smooth. Drizzle over bars. Let stand 5 minutes or until set. Cut bars at 45° angle into 1-inch slices. Place cookies on wire racks; cool completely.

PISTACHIO MACARONS

MAKES 16 TO 20 MACARONS

⅓ cup unsalted shelled pistachios (1½ ounces)

1½ cups powdered sugar

⅔ cup almond flour or meal

3 egg whites, at room temperature*

Green paste food coloring

¼ cup granulated sugar

Chocolate Ganache or Pistachio Filling (page 15)

For best results, separate the eggs while cold. Leave the egg whites at room temperature for 3 or 4 hours. Reserve yolks in refrigerator for another use.

1 Stack two cookie sheets; line top sheet with parchment paper. Repeat with two more cookie sheets. (Do not use insulated baking sheets.)

2 Place pistachios in food processor; pulse about 1 minute or until coarsely ground but not pasty. Add powdered sugar and almond flour; pulse 2 to 3 minutes or until well combined into very fine powder, scraping bowl occasionally. Sift mixture twice; discard any remaining large pieces.

3 Beat egg whites in large bowl with electric mixer on high speed until foamy. Add food coloring. Gradually add granulated sugar, beating on high speed 2 to 3 minutes or until stiff, shiny peaks form.

4 Add half of sifted pistachio mixture to egg whites. Stir with spatula to combine (about 12 strokes). Repeat with remaining pistachio mixture. Mix 15 strokes more by pressing against side of bowl and scooping from bottom until batter is smooth and shiny. Check consistency by dropping spoonful of batter onto plate. It should have a peak which quickly relaxes back into batter. Do not overmix or undermix.

5 Attach ½-inch plain piping tip to pastry bag. Scoop batter into bag. Pipe 1-inch circles about 2 inches apart onto prepared cookie sheets. Tap cookie sheets on flat surface to remove air bubbles. Let rest, uncovered, until tops harden slightly, about 15 minutes on dry days to 1 hour in

more humid conditions. Gently touch top of macaron to check. When batter does not stick, macarons are ready to bake.

6 Preheat oven to 375°F.** Place one sheet of macarons in oven. Bake 5 minutes. *Reduce oven temperature to 325°F.* Bake 10 to 13 minutes, checking at 5-minute intervals. If macarons begin to brown, cover loosely with foil and reduce oven temperature or prop oven door open slightly with wooden spoon. Repeat with remaining sheet.

7 Cool completely on cookie sheets on wire racks. If macarons appear to be sticking to parchment, lift parchment edges and spray pan underneath lightly with water. (Steam will help them release.)

8 Prepare desired filling(s). Match same size cookies; spread bottom macaron with filling and top with another. Store macarons in covered container in refrigerator up to 5 days. Freeze for longer storage.

**Oven temperature is crucial. Use an oven thermometer, if possible.

CHOCOLATE GANACHE: Place 4 ounces chopped semisweet or bittersweet chocolate in shallow bowl. Heat ½ cup whipping cream in small saucepan over low heat until bubbles form around edge. Pour cream over chocolate; let stand 5 minutes. Stir until smooth.

PISTACHIO FILLING: Combine 1 cup powdered sugar and ⅓ cup pistachios in food processor; process 2 to 3 minutes or until coarse paste forms, scraping bowl occasionally. Add 6 tablespoons softened butter and ½ teaspoon vanilla; pulse to combine.

OLD-FASHIONED OATMEAL COOKIES

MAKES 3 DOZEN COOKIES

2 cups old-fashioned oats

1⅓ cups all-purpose flour

¾ teaspoon baking soda

½ teaspoon baking powder

½ teaspoon salt

1 cup packed brown sugar

¾ cup (1½ sticks) butter, softened

¼ cup granulated sugar

1 egg

1 tablespoon honey

1 teaspoon vanilla

1 Preheat oven to 350°F. Line cookie sheets with parchment paper.

2 Combine oats, flour, baking soda, baking powder and salt in medium bowl.

3 Beat brown sugar, butter and granulated sugar in large bowl with electric mixer on medium speed until light and fluffy. Add egg, honey and vanilla; beat until well blended. Gradually add flour mixture, about ½ cup at a time; beat just until blended. Drop dough by heaping tablespoonfuls about 2 inches apart onto prepared cookie sheets.

4 Bake 11 to 15 minutes or until cookies are puffed and golden. Cool on cookie sheets 5 minutes. Remove to wire racks; cool completely.

HOLIDAY FRUIT DROPS

MAKES ABOUT 4 DOZEN COOKIES

¾ cup packed brown sugar

½ cup (1 stick) butter, softened

1 egg

1¼ cups all-purpose flour

1 teaspoon vanilla

½ teaspoon baking soda

½ teaspoon ground cinnamon

Pinch salt

1 cup (8 ounces) diced candied pineapple

1 cup (8 ounces) whole red and green candied cherries*

1 cup (8 ounces) chopped pitted dates

1 cup (6 ounces) semisweet chocolate chips

½ cup whole hazelnuts*

½ cup pecan halves*

½ cup coarsely chopped walnuts

*The cherries, hazelnuts and pecan halves are not chopped, but left whole.

1 Preheat oven to 325°F. Grease cookie sheets or line with parchment paper.

2 Beat brown sugar and butter in large bowl with electric mixer on medium speed 2 to 3 minutes or until creamy. Beat in egg until light and fluffy. Add flour, vanilla, baking soda, cinnamon and salt; beat just until blended. Stir in pineapple, cherries, dates, chocolate chips, hazelnuts, pecans and walnuts. Drop dough by rounded tablespoonfuls 2 inches apart onto prepared cookie sheets.

3 Bake 15 to 20 minutes or until firm and lightly browned around edges. Remove to wire racks; cool completely.

RICH AND BUTTERY COOKIES

MAKES 4 TO 5 DOZEN COOKIES

3½ cups all-purpose flour

2 teaspoons baking powder

¼ teaspoon salt

1 can (14 ounces) sweetened condensed milk

¾ cup (1½ sticks) butter, softened

2 eggs

1 tablespoon vanilla

Coarse sugar (optional)

1 Combine flour, baking powder and salt in small bowl; set aside.

2 Mix sweetened condensed milk, butter, eggs and vanilla in large bowl with electric mixer on low speed just until combined. Beat on medium speed 1 minute or until smooth. Add flour mixture; beat on low speed just until blended. Divide dough into thirds; shape into discs and wrap in plastic wrap. Refrigerate 2 hours or until firm.

3 Preheat oven to 350°F. Roll out one portion of dough on lightly floured surface to ⅛-inch thickness (keep remaining dough refrigerated). Cut with floured cookie cutter. Place 1 inch apart on ungreased cookie sheets. Reroll as necessary to use all dough. Sprinkle with coarse sugar, if desired.

4 Bake 9 to 11 minutes or until very lightly browned around edges. *Do not overbake.* Cool on cookie sheets 2 minutes. Remove to wire racks; cool completely.

TIP: These are great cookies for decorating. Dip them in chocolate and sprinkle with decors; drizzle with a powdered sugar glaze; or go all out with elaborate designs piped in royal icing. Unfrosted cookies freeze well, so you can bake them ahead and defrost them when you're ready to decorate.

DECADENT COCONUT MACAROONS

MAKES ABOUT 3 DOZEN COOKIES

1 package (14 ounces) flaked coconut

¾ cup sugar

6 tablespoons all-purpose flour

¼ teaspoon salt

4 egg whites

1 teaspoon vanilla

1 cup semisweet or bittersweet chocolate chips, melted

1 Preheat oven to 325°F. Line cookie sheets with parchment paper or grease and dust with flour.

2 Combine coconut, sugar, flour and salt in large bowl; mix well. Whisk egg whites and vanilla in small bowl. Stir into coconut mixture. Drop batter by tablespoonfuls 2 inches apart onto prepared cookie sheets.

3 Bake 20 minutes or until cookies are set and light golden brown. Immediately remove from cookie sheets to wire racks; cool completely.

4 Dip cooled cookies in melted chocolate; place on waxed paper-lined tray. Let stand at room temperature until chocolate is set. Store in tightly covered container at room temperature 1 week.

PEANUTTY DOUBLE CHIP COOKIES

½ cup (1 stick) butter, softened

¾ cup packed brown sugar

¾ cup granulated sugar

2 eggs

1 teaspoon baking soda

1 teaspoon vanilla

2 cups all-purpose flour

1 cup chunky peanut butter

1 cup semisweet or milk chocolate chips

1 cup peanut butter chips

1 Preheat oven to 350°F. Grease cookie sheets or line with parchment paper.

2 Beat butter and sugars in large bowl with electric mixer on medium speed until blended. Add eggs, baking soda and vanilla; beat until light. Blend in flour and peanut butter until well blended and stiff dough forms. Stir in chocolate and peanut butter chips.

3 Drop dough by heaping tablespoonfuls 2 inches apart onto prepared cookie sheets. Press cookies down with tines of fork to flatten slightly.

4 Bake 12 minutes or until set but not browned. *Do not overbake.* Remove to wire racks; cool completely.

THUMBPRINT COOKIES

MAKES 2 DOZEN COOKIES

½ cup (1 stick) butter, softened

½ (8-ounce) package cream cheese, softened

½ cup sugar

1 egg

1 egg white

1 teaspoon almond extract

½ teaspoon vanilla

2 cups all-purpose flour

½ teaspoon salt

Fruit spread, any flavor

1 Preheat oven to 350°F. Line cookie sheets with parchment paper.

2 Beat butter, cream cheese and sugar in large bowl with electric mixer on medium speed until light and fluffy. Add egg, egg white, almond extract and vanilla; beat until well blended. Add flour and salt; beat until well blended.

3 Roll dough into 24 (1-inch) balls. Place on prepared cookie sheets. Using back of small spoon or thumb, make indentation in center of each ball; fill with ½ teaspoon fruit spread.

4 Bake 12 to 15 minutes until cookies are firm and lightly browned on bottoms. Remove to wire racks; cool completely.

RASPBERRY MACARONS

MAKES 16 TO 20 MACARONS

1½ cups powdered sugar

1 cup almond flour or meal

3 egg whites, at room temperature*

1 tablespoon raspberry liqueur

Red paste food coloring

¼ cup granulated sugar

Raspberry jam or Chocolate Ganache (page 15)

For best results, separate the eggs while cold. Leave the egg whites at room temperature for 3 or 4 hours. Reserve yolks in refrigerator for another use.

1 Stack two cookie sheets; line top sheet with parchment paper. Repeat with two more cookie sheets. (Do not use insulated baking sheets.)

2 Place powdered sugar and almond flour in food processor. Pulse 2 to 3 minutes or until well combined into very fine powder, scraping bowl occasionally. Sift mixture twice. Discard any remaining large pieces.

3 Beat egg whites in large bowl with electric mixer on high speed until foamy. Add liqueur and food coloring. Gradually add granulated sugar, beating on high speed 2 to 3 minutes or until mixture forms stiff, shiny peaks.

4 Add half of sifted flour mixture to egg whites. Stir with spatula to combine (about 12 strokes). Repeat with remaining flour mixture. Mix about 15 strokes more by pressing against side of bowl and scooping from bottom until batter is smooth and shiny. Check consistency by dropping spoonful of batter onto plate. It should have a peak which quickly relaxes back into batter. Do not overmix or undermix.

5 Attach ½-inch plain piping tip to pastry bag. Scoop batter into bag. Pipe 1-inch circles about 2 inches apart onto prepared cookie sheets. Tap cookie sheets on flat surface to remove air bubbles. Let rest, uncovered, until tops harden slightly, about 15 minutes on dry days to 1 hour in more humid conditions. Gently touch top of macaron to check. When batter does not stick, macarons are ready to bake.

6 Preheat oven to 375°F.** Place one sheet of macarons in oven. Bake 5 minutes. *Reduce oven temperature to 325°F.* Bake 10 to 13 minutes, checking at 5-minute intervals. If macarons begin to brown, cover loosely with foil and reduce oven temperature or prop oven open slightly with wooden spoon. Repeat with remaining cookie sheet.

7 Cool completely on cookie sheets on wire racks. If macarons appear to be sticking to parchment, lift parchment edges and spray pan underneath lightly with water. (Steam will help them release.)

8 Match same size cookies; spread bottom macaron with raspberry jam and top with another. Store macarons in covered container in refrigerator up to 5 days. Freeze for longer storage.

**Oven temperature is crucial. Use an oven thermometer, if possible.

ALMOND CRESCENTS

MAKES ABOUT 5 DOZEN COOKIES

1 cup (2 sticks) butter, softened

1 cup powdered sugar

2 egg yolks

2½ cups all-purpose flour

1½ teaspoons almond extract

1 cup semisweet or bittersweet chocolate chips, melted

1 Preheat oven to 375°F. Line cookie sheets with parchment paper.

2 Beat butter, powdered sugar and egg yolks in large bowl with electric mixer on medium speed until light and fluffy. Beat in flour and almond extract until well blended. Shape dough into 1-inch balls. (If dough is too soft to handle, cover and refrigerate until firm.)

3 Roll balls into 2-inch-long ropes, tapering both ends. Curve ropes into crescent shapes. Place 2 inches apart on prepared cookie sheets.

4 Bake 8 to 10 minutes or until set and bottoms are very lightly browned. Remove to wire racks; cool completely.

5 Dip one end of each crescent in melted chocolate. Place on waxed paper; let stand until chocolate is set.

CHOCOLATE-DIPPED ORANGE LOGS

MAKES ABOUT 3 DOZEN COOKIES

1 cup (2 sticks) butter, softened

1 cup sugar

2 eggs

1½ teaspoons grated orange peel

1 teaspoon vanilla

½ teaspoon salt

3¼ cups all-purpose flour

1 package (12 ounces) semisweet chocolate chips

1 cup pecan pieces, finely chopped

1 Beat butter in large bowl with electric mixer on medium speed until smooth. Gradually beat in sugar; increase speed to high and beat until light and fluffy. Beat in eggs, one at a time, blending well after each addition. Beat in orange peel, vanilla and salt until blended. Gradually add flour on low speed until blended. (Dough will be crumbly.)

2 Gather dough together and press gently to form a ball. Flatten into a disc; wrap in plastic wrap and refrigerate until firm, at least 2 hours or overnight.

3 Preheat oven to 350°F. Shape dough into 1-inch balls. Roll balls on flat surface to form 3-inch logs about ½ inch thick. Place logs 1 inch apart on ungreased cookie sheets.

4 Bake about 15 minutes or until bottoms of cookies are golden brown. (Cookies will feel soft but will become crisp when cool.) Remove to wire racks; cool completely.

5 Melt chocolate chips in top of double boiler over hot, not boiling, water. Place chopped pecans in small bowl. Dip both ends of cookies in chocolate, scraping off excess. Dip chocolate-covered ends in pecans. Place on waxed paper-lined cookie sheets and let stand until chocolate is set, or refrigerate about 5 minutes to set chocolate.

FROSTED BUTTER COOKIES

MAKES ABOUT 3 DOZEN COOKIES

1½ cups (3 sticks) butter, softened

¾ cup granulated sugar

3 egg yolks

3 cups all-purpose flour

1 teaspoon baking powder

2 tablespoons orange juice

1 teaspoon vanilla

Buttercream Icing (recipe follows) or Meringue Powder Royal Icing (page 35)

1 Beat 1½ cups butter and granulated sugar in large bowl with electric mixer on medium-high speed until creamy. Add egg yolks; beat until blended. Add flour, baking powder, orange juice and 1 teaspoon vanilla; beat until well mixed. Shape dough into two discs; wrap in plastic wrap. Refrigerate 2 to 3 hours or until firm.

2 Preheat oven to 350°F. Roll out dough, half at a time, to ¼-inch thickness on well floured surface. Cut dough with cookie cutters. Place 1 inch apart on ungreased cookie sheets. Bake 6 to 10 minutes or until edges are golden brown. Remove to wire racks; cool completely.

3 Prepare desired icing; tint desired colors. Place each color into piping bag filled with desired tips. Decorate cookies.

BUTTERCREAM ICING: Beat 4 cups powdered sugar, ½ cup (1 stick) softened butter, 3 tablespoons milk and 2 teaspoons vanilla in large bowl with electric mixer on low speed until blended. Beat on medium-high speed until light and fluffy.

MERINGUE POWDER ROYAL ICING

MAKES ABOUT 2½ CUPS

¼ cup plus 2 tablespoons
   water

¼ cup meringue powder*

1 package (16 ounces)
   powdered sugar, sifted

*Meringue powder is available online
and where cake decorating supplies
are sold.

1 Beat water and meringue powder in medium bowl with electric mixer on low speed until well blended. Beat on high speed about 5 minutes or until stiff peaks form.

2 Beat in powdered sugar on low speed until well blended. Beat on high speed until icing is very stiff. Beat in additional water by teaspoonfuls until desired piping consistency is reached.

MAGICAL
CHOCOLATE

FESTIVE FUDGE BLOSSOMS

MAKES ABOUT 2½ DOZEN COOKIES

½ cup (1 stick) butter, softened

¾ cup sugar

1 egg

1 teaspoon vanilla

½ teaspoon salt

1½ cups all-purpose flour

½ cup unsweetened cocoa powder

1 cup finely chopped walnuts

30 chocolate star candies

1 Beat butter and sugar in large bowl with electric mixer on medium speed until light and fluffy. Add egg, vanilla and salt; beat until well blended. Add flour and cocoa; beat on low speed just until blended. Shape dough into a ball; wrap in plastic wrap and refrigerate 1 hour or until firm.

2 Preheat oven to 350°F. Line cookie sheets with parchment paper. Place walnuts in small bowl. Shape dough into ½-inch balls. Roll in walnuts; press gently into dough. Place 2 inches apart on prepared cookie sheets.

3 Bake 12 minutes or until puffed and nearly set. Place chocolate star in center of each cookie; bake 1 minute. Cool on cookie sheets 2 minutes. Remove to wire racks; cool completely.

DUTCH CHOCOLATE MERINGUES

MAKES ABOUT 6 DOZEN COOKIES

¼ cup finely chopped pecans

2½ tablespoons unsweetened cocoa powder (preferably Dutch process)

3 egg whites

¼ teaspoon salt

¾ cup granulated sugar

Powdered sugar

1 Preheat oven to 200°F. Line cookie sheets with foil; grease foil.

2 Combine pecans and cocoa in medium bowl.

3 Beat egg whites and salt in large bowl with electric mixer on high speed until light and foamy. Gradually add granulated sugar; beat until stiff peaks form.

4 Gently fold pecan mixture into egg white mixture with rubber spatula by gently cutting down to bottom of bowl, scraping up side of bowl, then folding over top of mixture.

5 Spoon batter into pastry bag fitted with large plain tip. Pipe 1-inch mounds 2 inches apart on prepared cookie sheets.

6 Bake 1 hour. Turn oven off. *Do not open oven door.* Let stand in oven about 2 hours or overnight.

7 When cookies are firm, carefully peel cookies from foil. Dust with powdered sugar. Store loosely covered at room temperature up to 2 days.

MERINGUE MUSHROOMS: Pipe same number of 1-inch-tall "stems" as mounds. Bake as directed in step 6. When cookies are firm, attach "stems" to "caps" with melted chocolate. Dust with sifted unsweetened cocoa powder.

HOT CHOCOLATE COOKIES

MAKES ABOUT 2 DOZEN COOKIES

½ cup sugar

½ cup (1 stick) butter, softened

¼ teaspoon salt

1 cup milk chocolate chips, melted, divided

1 cup all-purpose flour

Mini marshmallows, cut into small pieces

1 Preheat oven to 350°F. Lightly grease cookie sheets or line with parchment paper.

2 Beat sugar, butter and salt in large bowl with electric mixer on medium speed until well blended. Add ¼ cup melted chocolate; beat until well blended. Gradually add flour, beating well after each addition.

3 Shape dough by level tablespoonfuls into balls. (If dough is too soft, refrigerate 1 hour or until firm enough to handle.) Place 2 inches apart on prepared cookie sheets; flatten to ½-inch thickness.

4 Bake 15 to 17 minutes or until set. Cool on cookie sheets 5 minutes. Remove to wire racks; cool completely.

5 Spread about 1 teaspoon remaining melted chocolate onto each cookie. Sprinkle with marshmallow pieces; press gently into chocolate. Refrigerate at least 1 hour or until set.

REVERSE CHOCOLATE CHIP COOKIES

MAKES 3 DOZEN COOKIES

4 ounces unsweetened chocolate

2 cups all-purpose flour

1½ teaspoons baking powder

½ teaspoon salt

1½ cups packed brown sugar

¾ cup (1½ sticks) butter, softened

1 teaspoon vanilla

2 eggs

1 package (12 ounces) white chocolate chips

1 Preheat oven to 350°F. Melt unsweetened chocolate according to package directions; cool slightly.

2 Combine flour, baking powder and salt in medium bowl.

3 Beat brown sugar, butter and vanilla in large bowl with electric mixer on medium speed until light and fluffy. Add eggs one at a time; beat until well blended. Beat in melted chocolate. Gradually add flour mixture, mixing well after each addition. Stir in white chocolate chips. Drop by heaping tablespoonfuls 2 inches apart onto ungreased cookie sheets.

4 Bake 10 minutes or just until set. Cool on cookie sheets 1 minute. Remove to wire racks; cool completely.

VARIATION: Substitute 1 cup whole wheat flour for 1 cup of the all-purpose flour.

MARSHMALLOW SANDWICH COOKIES

MAKES ABOUT 2 DOZEN SANDWICH COOKIES

2 cups all-purpose flour

½ cup unsweetened cocoa powder

2 teaspoons baking soda

½ teaspoon salt

1½ cups sugar, divided

⅔ cup (10 tablespoons) butter, softened

¼ cup light corn syrup

1 egg

1 teaspoon vanilla

24 large marshmallows

1 Preheat oven to 350°F. Line cookie sheets with parchment paper or leave ungreased. Combine flour, cocoa, baking soda and salt in medium bowl.

2 Beat 1¼ cups sugar and butter in large bowl with electric mixer on medium-high speed until light and fluffy. Beat in corn syrup, egg and vanilla. Add flour mixture; beat until well blended. Cover and refrigerate dough 15 minutes or until firm enough to shape into balls.

3 Place remaining ¼ cup sugar in small bowl. Shape dough into 1-inch balls; roll in sugar to coat. Place cookies 3 inches apart on prepared cookie sheets.

4 Bake 10 to 11 minutes or until set. Cool on cookie sheets 3 minutes. Remove to wire racks; cool completely.

5 Place one cookie on microwavable plate. Top with one marshmallow. Microwave on HIGH about 10 seconds or until marshmallow is softened. Immediately place another cookie, flat side down, on top of hot marshmallow; press together. Repeat with remaining cookies and marshmallows.

MOCHA CRINKLES

MAKES ABOUT 3 DOZEN COOKIES

1⅓ cups packed brown sugar

½ cup vegetable oil

¼ cup sour cream

1 egg

1 teaspoon vanilla

1¾ cups all-purpose flour

¾ cup unsweetened cocoa powder

2 teaspoons instant coffee granules

1 teaspoon baking soda

¼ teaspoon salt

⅛ teaspoon black pepper

½ cup powdered sugar

1 Beat brown sugar and oil in large bowl with electric mixer on medium speed until well blended. Add sour cream, egg and vanilla; beat until well blended. Combine flour, cocoa, coffee granules, baking soda, salt and pepper in medium bowl; mix well. Beat into brown sugar mixture until well blended. Cover and refrigerate 3 to 4 hours.

2 Preheat oven to 350°F. Place powdered sugar in shallow bowl. Shape dough into 1-inch balls; roll in powdered sugar. Place 2 inches apart on ungreased cookie sheets.

3 Bake 10 to 12 minutes or until tops of cookies are firm. *Do not overbake.* Remove to wire racks; cool completely.

MEXICAN CHOCOLATE MACAROONS

MAKES ABOUT 2 DOZEN COOKIES

8 ounces semisweet chocolate, divided

1¾ cups plus ⅓ cup whole almonds, divided

¾ cup sugar

1 teaspoon ground cinnamon

½ teaspoon salt

2 egg whites

1 teaspoon vanilla

1 Preheat oven to 400°F. Grease cookie sheets or line with parchment paper.

2 Place 5 ounces of chocolate in food processor; process until coarsely chopped. Add 1¾ cups almonds, sugar, cinnamon and salt; pulse until mixture is finely ground. Add egg whites and vanilla; process just until mixture forms moist dough.

3 Shape dough into 1-inch balls. (Dough will be sticky.) Place 2 inches apart on prepared cookie sheets. Press 1 whole almond into center of each dough ball.

4 Bake 8 to 10 minutes or just until set. Cool on cookie sheets 2 minutes. Remove to wire racks; cool completely.

5 Melt remaining 3 ounces of chocolate. Place in small resealable food storage bag. Cut off small corner of bag. Drizzle chocolate over cookies. Let stand until set.

CHOCOLATE-RASPBERRY KOLACKY

MAKES ABOUT 1½ DOZEN COOKIES

2 ounces semisweet chocolate, coarsely chopped

1½ cups all-purpose flour

¼ teaspoon baking soda

¼ teaspoon salt

½ cup (1 stick) butter, softened

3 ounces cream cheese, softened

⅓ cup granulated sugar

1 teaspoon vanilla

Seedless raspberry jam

Powdered sugar

1 Place chocolate in small microwavable bowl. Microwave on HIGH 1 to 1½ minutes or until chocolate is melted, stirring after 1 minute. Let cool slightly.

2 Combine flour, baking soda and salt in small bowl; stir well. Beat butter and cream cheese in large bowl with electric mixer on medium speed until well blended. Beat in granulated sugar until light and fluffy. Beat in vanilla and melted chocolate. Gradually add flour mixture; beat on low speed just until blended. Divide dough in half; flatten each half into a disc. Wrap separately in plastic wrap. Refrigerate 1 to 2 hours or until firm.

3 Preheat oven to 375°F. Lightly grease cookie sheets. Roll out each dough disc on well-floured surface to ¼- to ⅛-inch thickness. Cut dough with 3-inch round cookie cutter. Place cutouts 2 inches apart on prepared cookie sheets. Place rounded ½ teaspoon jam in center of each circle. Bring three edges of dough circles up over jam; pinch edges together to seal, leaving center of triangle slightly open.

4 Bake 10 minutes or until set. Cool on cookie sheets 2 minutes. Remove to wire racks; cool completely. Sprinkle with powdered sugar. Store tightly covered in refrigerator; let stand 30 minutes at room temperature before serving.

CHOCOLATE HAZELNUT SANDWICH COOKIES

MAKES 2½ DOZEN COOKIES

¾ cup (1½ sticks) butter, softened

¾ cup sugar

3 egg yolks

1 teaspoon vanilla

2 cups all-purpose flour

¼ teaspoon salt

⅔ cup chocolate hazelnut spread

1 Beat butter and sugar in large bowl with electric mixer at medium speed 1 minute. Beat in egg yolks and vanilla until well blended. Add flour and salt; beat just until combined. Divide dough in half. Shape into 2 logs, each measuring 6×1½-inch. Wrap each log in plastic wrap. Refrigerate at least 2 hours or overnight.

2 Preheat oven to 350°F. Line cookie sheets with parchment paper. Unwrap dough. Cut logs into ⅛-inch-thick slices. Place cookies 1 inch apart on cookie sheets. Bake 10 to 12 minutes or until edges are lightly browned. Cool on cookie sheets 5 minutes. Remove to wire racks; cool completely.

3 Place chocolate hazelnut spread in small resealable food storage bag; cut off small corner of bag. Squeeze spread onto flat sides of half of cookies; top with remaining cookies.

TIP: These cookies are soft. Store in refrigerator for firmer cookies.

CHOCOLATE PRETZEL COOKIES

1 cup (2 sticks) butter, softened

¾ cup granulated sugar

½ cup unsweetened cocoa powder

1 egg

1 teaspoon vanilla

2 cups cake flour

1 teaspoon coarse salt, plus additional for garnish

4 ounces white chocolate, chopped

Pearl sugar

1 Beat butter and granulated sugar in large bowl with electric mixer on medium speed until light. Add cocoa, egg and vanilla; beat until well blended. Stir in flour and 1 teaspoon salt until well blended. Shape dough into a disc; wrap in plastic wrap. Refrigerate about 1 hour or until firm.

2 Preheat oven to 350°F. Line cookie sheets with parchment paper. Roll tablespoonfuls of dough into 12-inch ropes; shape into pretzels and place on prepared cookie sheets 2 inches apart. Bake 7 to 8 minutes or until firm. Cool on cookie sheets 5 minutes. Remove to wire racks; cool completely.

3 Place cookies on parchment paper. Melt white chocolate according to package directions. Drizzle over cookies; sprinkle with additional salt and pearl sugar. Let stand until white chocolate is set.

CHOCOLATE SURPRISE COOKIES

MAKES ABOUT 3½ DOZEN COOKIES

2¾ cups all-purpose flour

¾ cup unsweetened cocoa powder

½ teaspoon baking powder

½ teaspoon baking soda

½ teaspoon salt

1 cup (2 sticks) butter, softened

1½ cups packed brown sugar

½ cup plus 1 tablespoon granulated sugar, divided

2 eggs

1 teaspoon vanilla

1 cup chopped pecans, divided

1 package (9 ounces) caramels coated in milk chocolate

3 ounces white chocolate, coarsely chopped

1 Preheat oven to 375°F. Combine flour, cocoa, baking powder, baking soda and salt in medium bowl.

2 Beat butter, brown sugar and ½ cup granulated sugar with electric mixer on medium speed until light and fluffy; beat in eggs and vanilla. Gradually add flour mixture and ½ cup pecans; beat until well blended. Cover dough; refrigerate 15 minutes or until firm enough to roll into balls.

3 Place remaining ½ cup pecans and 1 tablespoon granulated sugar in shallow dish. Roll tablespoonful of dough around 1 caramel candy, covering completely; press one side into nut mixture. Place, nut side up, on ungreased cookie sheet. Repeat with remaining dough and candies, placing 3 inches apart.

4 Bake 10 to 12 minutes or until set and slightly cracked. Cool on cookie sheets 2 minutes. Remove to wire racks; cool completely.

5 Melt white chocolate according to package directions. Place in small resealable food storage bag. Cut off small corner of bag. Drizzle white chocolate over cookies. Let stand about 30 minutes or until chocolate is set.

SUPER CHOCOLATE COOKIES

MAKES ABOUT 20 COOKIES

2 cups all-purpose flour

⅓ cup unsweetened cocoa powder

1 teaspoon baking soda

½ teaspoon salt

1⅓ cups packed brown sugar

1 cup (2 sticks) butter, softened

2 eggs

2 teaspoons vanilla

1 cup candy-coated chocolate pieces

1 cup dried cranberries, dried cherries and raisins

¾ cup salted peanuts

1 Preheat oven to 350°F. Combine flour, cocoa, baking soda and salt in medium bowl.

2 Beat brown sugar and butter in large bowl with electric mixer on medium speed until light and fluffy. Add eggs and vanilla; beat until well blended. Gradually add flour mixture on low speed until blended. Stir in chocolate pieces, cranberries and peanuts.

3 Drop dough by ¼ cupfuls 3 inches apart onto ungreased cookie sheets. Flatten slightly with fingertips.

4 Bake 13 to 15 minutes or until almost set. Cool on cookie sheets 2 minutes. Remove to wire racks; cool completely.

CHOCOLATE MACARONS

MAKES 16 TO 20 MACARONS

1 cup powdered sugar

⅔ cup almond flour or meal

3 tablespoons unsweetened cocoa powder

3 egg whites, at room temperature*

¼ cup granulated sugar

Chocolate Ganache (page 15), chocolate-hazelnut spread or raspberry jam

*For best results, separate the eggs while cold. Leave the egg whites at room temperature for 3 or 4 hours. Reserve yolks in refrigerator for another use.

1 Stack two cookie sheets; line top sheet with parchment paper. Repeat with two more cookie sheets. (Do not use insulated baking sheets.)

2 Place powdered sugar, almond flour and cocoa in food processor. Pulse 2 to 3 minutes or until well combined into very fine powder, scraping bowl occasionally. Sift mixture twice. Discard any remaining large pieces.

3 Beat egg whites in large bowl with electric mixer on high speed until foamy. Gradually add granulated sugar, beating on high speed 2 to 3 minutes or until mixture forms stiff, shiny peaks.

4 Add half of flour mixture to egg whites. Stir with spatula to combine (about 12 strokes). Repeat with remaining flour mixture. Mix about 15 strokes more by pressing against side of bowl and scooping from bottom until batter is smooth and shiny. Check consistency by dropping spoonful of batter onto plate. It should have a peak which quickly relaxes back into batter. Do not overmix or undermix.

5 Attach ½-inch plain piping tip to pastry bag. Scoop batter into bag. Pipe 1-inch circles about 2 inches apart onto prepared cookie sheets. Tap cookie sheets on flat surface to remove air bubbles. Let rest, uncovered, until tops harden slightly, about 15 minutes on dry days to 1 hour in more humid conditions. Gently touch top of macaron to check. When batter does not stick, macarons are ready to bake.

6 Meanwhile, preheat oven to 375°F.* Place one sheet in oven. Bake 5 minutes. *Reduce oven temperature to 325°F.* Bake 10 to 13 minutes, checking at 5-minute intervals. If macarons begin to brown, cover loosely with foil and reduce oven temperature or prop oven door open slightly with wooden spoon. Repeat with remaining cookie sheet.

7 Cool completely on cookie sheets on wire racks. If macarons appear to be sticking to parchment, lift parchment edges and spray pan underneath lightly with water. (Steam will help them release.)

8 Match same size cookies; spread bottom macaron with ganache and top with another. Store macarons in covered container in refrigerator up to 5 days.

**Oven temperature is crucial. Use an oven thermometer, if possible.

DEEP DARK CHOCOLATE CHIP COOKIES

MAKES ABOUT 2½ DOZEN COOKIES

2 packages (12 ounces each) semisweet or bittersweet chocolate chips, divided

½ cup (1 stick) butter, cut into pieces

2 eggs

1 teaspoon vanilla

¾ cup plus 2 tablespoons sugar

⅔ cup all-purpose flour

2 tablespoons unsweetened Dutch process cocoa powder

1 teaspoon baking powder

¼ teaspoon salt

1 Lightly grease cookie sheets or line with parchment paper.

2 Combine 1 package chocolate chips and butter in large microwavable bowl. Microwave on HIGH 30 seconds; stir. Repeat as necessary until chips are melted and mixture is smooth. Cool slightly.

3 Beat eggs and vanilla in large bowl with electric mixer on medium speed until blended and frothy. Add sugar; beat on high speed about 3 minutes or until thick and pale. Add chocolate mixture; beat until blended. Add flour, cocoa, baking powder and salt; beat until blended. Stir in remaining chocolate chips. (Dough will be soft.)

4 Drop dough by rounded tablespoonfuls about 2 inches apart onto prepared cookie sheets. Refrigerate 30 minutes.

5 Preheat oven to 325°F. Bake 16 to 20 minutes or until cookies are firm to the touch. Cool on cookie sheets 2 minutes. Remove to wire racks; cool completely.

SUGAR &
SPICE

GINGERBREAD PEOPLE

MAKES ABOUT 4 DOZEN COOKIES

½ cup (1 stick) butter, softened

½ cup packed brown sugar

⅓ cup water

⅓ cup molasses

1 egg

4 cups all-purpose flour

2 teaspoons baking soda

1 teaspoon ground ginger

½ teaspoon salt

½ teaspoon ground allspice

½ teaspoon ground cinnamon

½ teaspoon ground cloves

Assorted icings and candies

1 Beat butter and brown sugar in large bowl with electric mixer on medium speed until creamy. Add water, molasses and egg; beat until blended. Add flour, baking soda, ginger, salt, allspice, cinnamon and cloves; beat until well blended. Shape dough into a disc; wrap tightly with plastic wrap. Refrigerate 2 hours or until firm.

2 Preheat oven to 350°F. Grease cookie sheets or line with parchment paper. Roll out dough on lightly floured surface with lightly floured rolling pin to ⅛-inch thickness. Cut out shapes with cookie cutter. Place cutouts 2 inches apart on prepared cookie sheets.

3 Bake 12 to 15 minutes or until set. Cool on cookie sheets 1 minute. Remove to wire racks; cool completely. Decorate as desired. Store in airtight containers.

GINGER MOLASSES SPICE COOKIES

2 cups all-purpose flour

1½ teaspoons ground ginger

1 teaspoon baking soda

½ teaspoon salt

½ teaspoon ground cinnamon

½ teaspoon ground cloves

1¼ cups sugar, divided

¾ cup (1½ sticks) butter, softened

¼ cup molasses

1 egg

1 Preheat oven to 375°F. Combine flour, ginger, baking soda, salt, cinnamon and cloves in medium bowl.

2 Beat 1 cup sugar and butter in large bowl with electric mixer on medium speed until light and fluffy. Add molasses and egg; beat until well blended. Gradually beat in flour mixture on low speed just until blended.

3 Place remaining ¼ cup sugar in shallow bowl. Shape dough by teaspoonfuls into balls; roll in sugar to coat. Place 1 inch apart on ungreased cookie sheets.

4 Bake 7 to 8 minutes or until almost set. Cool on cookie sheets 2 minutes. Remove to wire racks; cool completely.

TIP: For larger cookies, drop by tablespoonfuls onto cookie sheets. Bake 10 to 11 minutes or until almost set. Makes about 2½ dozen cookies.

FESTIVE LEBKUCHEN

MAKES 1 DOZEN COOKIES

1 cup packed brown sugar

¼ cup honey

3 tablespoons butter

1 egg

Grated peel and juice of 1 lemon

3 cups all-purpose flour

2 teaspoons ground allspice

½ teaspoon baking soda

½ teaspoon salt

White decorating frosting

1 Combine brown sugar, honey and butter in medium saucepan. Cook over low heat until sugar and butter are melted, stirring constantly. Pour into large bowl. Cool 30 minutes.

2 Add egg, lemon peel and juice; beat 2 minutes with electric mixer on high speed. Stir in flour, allspice, baking soda and salt until well blended. Cover and refrigerate overnight or up to 3 days.

3 Preheat oven to 350°F. Grease cookie sheets or line with parchment paper. Roll out dough to ½-inch thickness on lightly floured surface with lightly floured rolling pin. Cut out with 3-inch cookie cutters. Transfer to prepared cookie sheets.

4 Bake 15 to 18 minutes until edges are lightly browned. Cool on cookie sheets 1 minute. Remove to wire racks; cool completely. Decorate with white frosting. Store in airtight container.

GERMAN SPICE COOKIES

MAKES 2½ DOZEN COOKIES

2 cups all-purpose flour

1½ teaspoons ground cinnamon

½ teaspoon baking soda

½ teaspoon ground cloves

¼ teaspoon salt

1⅓ cups blanched almonds

1 cup granulated sugar

½ cup (1 stick) butter, melted

2 eggs

2 teaspoons grated lemon peel

1 teaspoon anise seed (optional)

½ teaspoon almond extract

2 tablespoons finely minced crystallized ginger*

½ cup powdered sugar

*Semisoft sugar-coated ginger slices are available at natural foods or specialty stores. If using the small dry cubes of ginger, steep the cubes in boiling hot water a few minutes to soften, then drain, pat dry and mince.

1 Preheat oven to 350°F. Sift flour, cinnamon, baking soda, cloves and salt into medium bowl. Place almonds in food processor or blender; pulse until coarse meal forms.

2 Beat granulated sugar, butter and eggs in large bowl with electric mixer on medium speed until blended. Add lemon peel, anise seed, if desired, and almond extract; mix well. Gradually add flour mixture on low speed until blended. (Dough will be stiff.) Fold in ginger and almond meal with rubber spatula.

3 Shape dough into 1-inch balls; place 2 inches apart on ungreased cookie sheets.

4 Bake 15 minutes or until bottoms are lightly browned and tops just start to crack. Cool on cookie sheets 5 minutes. Place powdered sugar in shallow dish. Gently roll warm cookies in powdered sugar. Cool completely on wire rack.

TIP: To allow the flavors to blend, make these cookies 2 to 3 weeks in advance. Store at room temperature in an airtight container.

MOLASSES SPICE COOKIES

MAKES ABOUT 6 DOZEN COOKIES

2 cups all-purpose flour

2 teaspoons baking soda

1 teaspoon ground ginger

1 teaspoon ground cinnamon

1 teaspoon ground cloves

¼ teaspoon salt

¼ teaspoon dry mustard

1 cup granulated sugar

¾ cup shortening

¼ cup molasses

1 egg

½ cup granulated brown sugar* or turbinado sugar

*Granulated brown sugar is brown sugar that has been processed to have a light, dry texture similar to granulated sugar. It can be found in the baking aisles of most supermarkets.

1 Preheat oven to 375°F. Grease cookie sheets or line with parchment paper.

2 Combine flour, baking soda, ginger, cinnamon, cloves, salt and mustard in medium bowl.

3 Beat granulated sugar and shortening in large bowl with electric mixer at medium speed 5 minutes or until light and fluffy. Add molasses and egg; beat until blended. Add flour mixture, beat on low speed just until blended.

4 Place granulated brown sugar in shallow dish. Shape dough into 1-inch balls; roll in sugar to coat. Place 2 inches apart on prepared cookie sheets.

5 Bake 15 minutes or until lightly browned. Cool on cookie sheets 2 minutes. Remove to wire racks; cool completely.

HONEY SPICE BALLS

MAKES ABOUT 2½ DOZEN COOKIES

½ cup (1 stick) butter, softened

½ cup packed brown sugar

1 egg

1 tablespoon honey

1 teaspoon vanilla

2 cups all-purpose flour

½ teaspoon baking powder

½ teaspoon ground cinnamon

¼ teaspoon salt

¼ teaspoon ground nutmeg

½ cup quick oats

1 Preheat oven to 350°F. Grease cookie sheets or line with parchment paper.

2 Beat butter and brown sugar in large bowl with electric mixer on medium speed until creamy. Add egg, honey and vanilla; beat until light and fluffy. Stir in flour, baking powder, cinnamon, salt and nutmeg on low speed until well blended.

3 Place oats in small bowl. Shape tablespoonfuls of dough into balls; roll in oats. Place 2 inches apart on prepared cookie sheets.

4 Bake 15 to 18 minutes or until tops crack slightly. Cool on cookie sheets 1 minute. Remove to wire racks; cool completely. Store in airtight container.

BAKLAVA

MAKES ABOUT 32 PIECES

4 cups walnuts, shelled pistachios and/or slivered almonds (1 pound)

1¼ cups sugar, divided

2 teaspoons ground cinnamon

½ teaspoon salt

¼ teaspoon ground cloves

1 package (16 ounces) frozen phyllo dough, thawed

1 cup (2 sticks) butter, melted

1½ cups water

¾ cup honey

2 (2-inch-long) strips lemon peel

1 tablespoon fresh lemon juice

1 whole cinnamon stick

3 whole cloves

1 Place 2 cups nuts in food processor. Pulse until nuts are finely chopped, but not pasty. Remove from container. Repeat with remaining nuts.

2 Combine nuts, ½ cup sugar, cinnamon, salt and ground cloves in medium bowl; mix well.

3 Unroll phyllo dough and place on large sheet of waxed paper. Trim phyllo to 13×9 inches. Cover phyllo with plastic wrap and damp, clean kitchen towel. (Phyllo dough dries out quickly.)

4 Preheat oven to 325°F. Brush 13×9-inch baking dish with some of melted butter.

5 Place 1 phyllo sheet in bottom of dish, folding in edges if too long; brush surface with butter. Repeat with 7 more phyllo sheets, brushing surface of each sheet with butter. Sprinkle about ½ cup nut mixture evenly over layered phyllo.

6 Top nuts with 3 more layers of phyllo, brushing each sheet with butter. Sprinkle another ½ cup nut mixture on top. Repeat layering and brushing of 3 phyllo sheets with ½ cup nut mixture until there are a total of eight 3-sheet layers. Top final layer of nut mixture with remaining 8 phyllo sheets, brushing each sheet with butter.

7 Score baklava lengthwise into 4 equal sections, then score diagonally at 1½-inch intervals to form diamonds. Sprinkle top lightly with some water to prevent top phyllo from curling up during baking. Bake 50 to 60 minutes or until golden brown.

8 Meanwhile, combine 1½ cups water, remaining ¾ cup sugar, honey, lemon peel, lemon juice, cinnamon stick and whole cloves in medium saucepan. Bring to a boil over high heat. Reduce heat to low; simmer 15 minutes.

9 Strain hot syrup; drizzle evenly over hot baklava. Cool completely. Cut into diamonds along score lines.

CARDAMOM CHOCOLATE SANDWICHES

MAKES ABOUT 1 DOZEN SANDWICH COOKIES

1½ cups all-purpose flour

1 teaspoon ground cardamom

½ teaspoon baking soda

½ teaspoon salt

1¼ cups (2½ sticks) butter, softened, divided

¾ cup packed dark brown sugar

1 egg

Pearl sugar or sparkling sugar

1 cup dark chocolate chips *or* 4 ounces bittersweet chocolate, chopped

2 cups powdered sugar

2 tablespoons cream or milk

1 Combine flour, cardamom, baking soda and salt in small bowl. Beat ¾ cup butter and brown sugar in large bowl with electric mixer on medium speed until light and fluffy. Beat in egg. Add flour mixture; beat on low speed just until blended. Shape dough into a disc; wrap with plastic wrap. Refrigerate 1 hour or until firm. (Dough may be kept refrigerated up to 3 days.)

2 Preheat oven to 300°F. Line cookie sheets with parchment paper. Roll out dough on well-floured surface ⅛ inch thick. Cut out 2-inch circles; place on prepared cookie sheets. Sprinkle half of cookies with pearl sugar. Bake 7 to 8 minutes or until cookies are set and lightly browned around edges. Cool on cookie sheets 2 minutes. Remove to wire racks; cool completely.

3 Heat chocolate chips in medium microwavable bowl on HIGH 1½ minutes or until melted, stirring after 1 minute.

4 Beat remaining ½ cup butter and powdered sugar in large bowl with electric mixer at medium-low speed about 1 minute or until creamy. Beat on medium speed until fluffy. Add melted chocolate and cream; beat on medium-high speed about 1 minute or until well blended and fluffy. Spread filling on flat side of one plain cookie; top with decorated cookie. Repeat with remaining cookies and filling.

CAPPUCCINO SPICE COOKIES

MAKES ABOUT 3½ DOZEN COOKIES

2½ teaspoons instant coffee granules

1 tablespoon boiling water

2⅔ cups all-purpose flour

1 teaspoon baking soda

¾ teaspoon ground cinnamon

½ teaspoon salt

¼ teaspoon ground nutmeg or ground cloves

1 cup (2 sticks) butter, softened

1 cup packed brown sugar

½ cup granulated sugar

2 eggs

1 teaspoon vanilla

1½ packages (12 ounces each) bittersweet or semisweet chocolate chips

1 Preheat oven to 375°F. Dissolve coffee granules in boiling water in small bowl.

2 Combine flour, baking soda, cinnamon, salt and nutmeg in medium bowl.

3 Beat butter, brown sugar and granulated sugar in large bowl with electric mixer on medium speed until light and fluffy. Add eggs, coffee and vanilla; beat until well blended. Gradually add flour mixture on low speed until well blended. Stir in chocolate chips. Drop dough by rounded tablespoonfuls 2 inches apart onto ungreased cookie sheets.

4 Bake 8 to 10 minutes or until set. Cool on cookie sheets 1 minute. Remove to wire racks; cool completely.

CAPPUCCINO SPICE MINIS: For smaller cookies, prepare dough as directed above. Drop dough by rounded teaspoonfuls 2 inches apart onto ungreased cookie sheets. Bake 7 minutes or until set. Makes about 7 dozen mini cookies.

TRIPLE GINGER COOKIES

MAKES 3 DOZEN COOKIES

2 cups all-purpose flour

2 teaspoons baking soda

1 teaspoon ground ginger

½ teaspoon salt

¾ cup (1½ sticks) butter

1¼ cups sugar, divided

¼ cup molasses

1 egg

1 tablespoon finely minced fresh ginger

1 tablespoon finely minced crystallized ginger*

Semisoft sugar-coated ginger slices are available at natural foods or specialty stores. If using the small dry cubes of ginger, steep the cubes in boiling hot water a few minutes to soften, then drain, pat dry and mince.

1 Line cookie sheets with parchment paper or lightly grease. Whisk flour, baking soda, ground ginger and salt in medium bowl.

2 Melt butter in small heavy saucepan over low heat; pour into large bowl and cool slightly. Add 1 cup sugar, molasses and egg; beat with electric mixer on medium speed until well blended. Gradually add flour mixture on low speed. Add fresh ginger and crystallized ginger; mix just until blended. Cover; refrigerate 1 hour.

3 Preheat oven to 375°F. Place remaining ¼ cup sugar in small bowl. Roll dough into 1-inch balls; roll in sugar. Place 3 inches apart on prepared cookie sheets. (If dough is very sticky, drop by teaspoonfuls into sugar to coat.)

4 For chewy cookies, bake 7 minutes or until edges just start to brown. For crisper cookies, bake 9 to 11 minutes. Cool on cookie sheets 1 minute. Remove to wire racks; cool completely.

VARIATION: Roll dough in plastic food wrap to form a log. Refrigerate up to 1 week or freeze up to 2 months until needed for baking. To bake, bring the dough nearly to room temperature and slice. Dip the tops in sugar and bake as instructed.

SHORT & SWEET

CHOCOLATE CHIP SHORTBREAD

MAKES ABOUT 1 DOZEN COOKIES

½ cup (1 stick) butter, softened

½ cup granulated sugar

2 tablespoons packed brown sugar

1 teaspoon vanilla

1 cup all-purpose flour

½ teaspoon salt

½ cup plus 2 tablespoons mini semisweet chocolate chips, divided

1 Preheat oven to 350°F. Spray 8- or 9-inch square baking pan with nonstick cooking spray.

2 Beat butter and sugars in large bowl with electric mixer on medium speed until light and fluffy. Beat in vanilla. Add flour and salt; beat on low speed until combined. Stir in ½ cup chocolate chips. Press dough into prepared pan. Sprinkle with remaining 2 tablespoons chocolate chips; press lightly into dough.

3 Bake 15 to 17 minutes or until edges are golden brown. Cool completely in pan on wire rack. Cut into rectangles.

ORANGE SHORTBREAD

MAKES 2½ DOZEN COOKIES

1 cup (2 sticks) butter, softened

⅔ cup powdered sugar

1 tablespoon grated orange peel

¼ teaspoon salt

½ teaspoon orange extract

2 cups all-purpose flour

Orange Frosting (recipe follows)

1 Preheat oven to 300°F.

2 Beat butter and sugar in large bowl with electric mixer on medium speed until creamy. Beat in orange peel, salt and orange extract. Add flour, ½ cup at a time, beating just until blended.

3 Shape dough into 30 balls, about 1 tablespoon each. Place on ungreased cookie sheets; flatten balls to ⅓-inch thickness.

4 Bake 15 to 20 minutes or until set. Cool on cookie sheets 5 minutes. Remove to wire racks; cool completely.

5 Prepare Orange Frosting; spread on cookies. Let stand 30 minutes or until frosting is set.

ORANGE FROSTING

1½ cups powdered sugar

¼ cup (½ stick) butter, softened

2 tablespoons orange juice

1 teaspoon grated orange peel

⅛ teaspoon salt

Beat sugar and butter in large bowl with electric mixer on medium speed until creamy. Add orange juice, orange peel and salt; beat on medium-high speed until fluffy.

LEMONY BUTTER COOKIES

MAKES ABOUT 2 DOZEN COOKIES

½ cup (1 stick) butter, softened

½ cup granulated sugar

1 egg

2 tablespoons fresh lemon juice

1 tablespoon grated lemon peel

½ teaspoon baking powder

½ teaspoon salt

1½ cups all-purpose flour

Coarse decorating sugar (optional)

1 Beat butter and granulated sugar in large bowl with electric mixer on medium speed until creamy. Beat in egg until light and fluffy. Add lemon juice, lemon peel, baking powder and salt; beat until blended. Gradually add flour on low speed. Wrap in plastic wrap; refrigerate about 2 hours or until firm.

2 Preheat oven to 350°F. Roll dough, a small portion at a time, on well-floured surface to ¼-inch thickness. (Keep remaining dough in refrigerator.) Cut dough with 3-inch round or fluted cookie cutter. Transfer cutouts to ungreased cookie sheets. Sprinkle with coarse sugar, if desired.

3 Bake 8 to 10 minutes or until edges are lightly browned. Cool on cookie sheets 1 minute. Remove to wire racks; cool completely.

VARIATION: Instead of rolling out the dough, shape it into ½-inch balls. Dip the tops in coarse decorating or pearl sugar and flatten slightly. Bake about 10 minutes or until set but not browned. Cool on cookie sheets 1 minute. Remove to wire rack; cool completely.

DANISH ORANGE COOKIES (ORANGESMEKAGER)

MAKES ABOUT 2½ DOZEN BARS

½ cup (1 stick) butter, softened

¼ cup granulated sugar

1 egg

½ teaspoon orange extract

2 tablespoons grated orange peel

1½ cups all-purpose flour

4 ounces semisweet chocolate, chopped

White sugar pearls or other decors

1 Beat butter and granulated sugar in large bowl with electric mixer on medium speed until light and fluffy. Beat in egg, orange extract and orange peel until well blended. Gradually add flour, beating on low speed until well blended. Shape dough into a disc; wrap in plastic wrap and refrigerate 1 hour or until firm.

2 Preheat oven to 375°F. Line cookie sheets with parchment paper.

3 Roll out dough on lightly floured surface with floured rolling pin to ¼-inch thickness. Cut dough into 2×1-inch bars. Place bars 2 inches apart on prepared cookie sheets. Gently press dough trimmings together; reroll and cut out more cookies.

4 Bake 10 minutes or until lightly browned. Remove cookies to wire racks; cool completely.

5 Melt chocolate in microwavable bowl on MEDIUM (50%) 1½ to 2 minutes, stirring occasionally. Dip half of each cookie into chocolate, scraping excess on bottoms back into bowl. Place cookies on waxed paper; sprinkle with sugar pearls. Let stand at room temperature 1 hour or until set. Store tightly covered between sheets of waxed paper at room temperature.

CHOCOLATE CHIP SHORTBREAD WITH EARL GREY GLAZE

MAKES ABOUT 2½ DOZEN COOKIES

1 cup (2 sticks) butter, softened

½ cup sugar

1 teaspoon grated orange peel

2 cups all-purpose flour

¼ cup cornstarch

¼ teaspoon salt

½ cup mini chocolate chips

Earl Grey Glaze (recipe follows)

1 Preheat oven to 300°F. Beat butter, sugar and orange peel in bowl of electric stand mixer on low speed until combined. Gradually beat in flour, cornstarch and salt until blended. Stir in chocolate chips; mix on low speed 30 seconds or until combined.

2 Roll dough into ¼-inch-thick rectangle on lightly floured board. Cut dough lengthwise into 4 rows and diagonally into 8 rows. Place shortbread 1 inch apart on ungreased cookie sheets.

3 Bake 15 to 20 minutes or until bottoms begin to brown. Cool on cookie sheets 5 minutes. Remove to wire racks; cool completely.

4 Prepare glaze. Drizzle over shortbread.

EARL GREY GLAZE

¼ cup boiling water

3 bags Earl Grey Tea

1 cup powdered sugar

1 tablespoon butter, softened

1 Pour boiling water over tea bags; let steep 3 to 5 minutes. Remove tea bags.

2 Whisk powdered sugar and butter in small bowl until well blended. Gradually stir in enough tea to make glaze thin enough to drizzle.

LINZER SANDWICH COOKIES

MAKES ABOUT 2 DOZEN SANDWICH COOKIES

1⅔ cups all-purpose flour

¼ teaspoon baking powder

¼ teaspoon salt

¾ cup granulated sugar

½ cup (1 stick) butter, softened

1 egg

1 teaspoon vanilla

Powdered sugar (optional)

Seedless red raspberry jam

1 Combine flour, baking powder and salt in medium bowl. Beat granulated sugar and butter in large bowl with electric mixer on medium speed until light and fluffy. Beat in egg and vanilla until blended. Gradually add flour mixture on low speed until dough forms. Divide dough in half. Wrap each half in plastic wrap; refrigerate 2 hours or until firm.

2 Preheat oven to 375°F. Roll out half of dough on lightly floured surface to ¼-inch thickness. Cut out circles with 1½-inch floured scalloped or plain round cookie cutters. (If dough becomes too soft, refrigerate several minutes before continuing.) Place cutouts 2 inches apart on ungreased cookie sheets.

3 Roll out remaining half of dough and cut out circles. Cut 1-inch centers of different shapes from circles. Place 2 inches apart on ungreased cookie sheets.

4 Bake 7 to 9 minutes or until edges are lightly browned. Cool cookies on cookie sheets 2 minutes. Remove to wire racks; cool completely.

5 Sprinkle powdered sugar over cookies with cutouts, if desired. Spread jam on flat sides of whole cookies; top with sugar-dusted cookies. Store tightly covered at room temperature, or freeze up to 3 months.

BUTTERY ALMOND SHORTBREAD

MAKES ABOUT 3½ DOZEN COOKIES

1¼ cups all-purpose flour

½ teaspoon baking powder

¼ teaspoon salt

10 tablespoons butter, softened

¾ cup sugar

1 egg

1 teaspoon vanilla

¾ cup slivered almonds, finely chopped

½ cup slivered almonds (optional)

1 Preheat oven to 350°F. Grease cookie sheets or line with parchment paper. Combine flour, baking powder and salt in small bowl.

2 Beat butter in large bowl with electric mixer on medium speed until smooth. Gradually beat in sugar until blended. Increase speed to high; beat until light and fluffy. Beat in egg and vanilla. Gradually stir in flour mixture until blended. Stir in chopped almonds.

3 Drop rounded teaspoonfuls of dough 2 inches apart onto prepared cookie sheets. Press several slivered almonds into dough of each cookie, if desired.

4 Bake 12 minutes or until edges are golden brown. Cool on cookie sheets 5 minutes. Remove to wire racks; cool completely. Store in airtight container.

ORANGE-ALMOND SABLES

MAKES ABOUT 2 DOZEN COOKIES

¾ cup whole blanched almonds, toasted*

1¾ cups all-purpose flour

¼ teaspoon salt

1½ cups powdered sugar

1 cup (2 sticks) butter, softened

1 tablespoon finely grated orange peel

1 tablespoon almond-flavored liqueur *or* 1 teaspoon almond extract

1 egg, beaten

To toast almonds, spread in single layer on baking sheet. Bake in preheated 350°F oven 8 to 10 minutes or until golden brown, stirring frequently. Cool completely.

1 Preheat oven to 375°F. Reserve 24 whole almonds. Place remaining almonds in food processor; pulse until ground but not pasty. Transfer to medium bowl; stir in flour and salt.

2 Beat powdered sugar and butter in large bowl with electric mixer on medium speed until light and fluffy. Beat in orange peel and liqueur. Gradually add flour mixture on low speed; beat until well blended.

3 Roll dough on lightly floured surface with lightly floured rolling pin to ¼-inch thickness. Cut dough with floured 2½-inch fluted or round cookie cutter. Place cutouts 2 inches apart on ungreased cookie sheets. Press one reserved whole almond in center of each cutout. Lightly brush tops of cutouts with beaten egg.

4 Bake 10 to 12 minutes or until light golden brown. Let cookies stand on cookie sheets 1 minute. Remove to wire racks; cool completely. Store tightly covered at room temperature, or freeze up to 3 months.

SCOTTISH SHORTBREAD

MAKES ABOUT 4 DOZEN BARS OR 24 WEDGES

5 cups all-purpose flour

1 cup rice flour

½ teaspoon salt

2 cups (4 sticks) butter, softened

1 cup sugar

1 Preheat oven to 325°F. Sift together flours and salt in medium bowl. Beat butter and sugar in large bowl with electric mixer on medium speed until creamy. Blend in three fourths of flour until mixture resembles fine crumbs. Stir in remaining flour by hand.

2 Press dough firmly into ungreased 15×10-inch jelly-roll pan or two 9-inch fluted tart pans; crimp and flute edges of dough in jelly-roll pan, if desired.

3 Bake 40 to 45 minutes or until light brown. Place pan on wire rack. Cut into bars or wedges while warm. Cool completely.

CARIBBEAN CRUNCH SHORTBREAD

MAKES ABOUT 2 DOZEN COOKIES

1 cup (2 sticks) butter, softened

½ cup powdered sugar

2 tablespoons packed brown sugar

¼ teaspoon salt

2 cups all-purpose flour

1 cup diced dried tropical fruit mix, such as pineapple, mango and papaya

1 Beat butter, sugars and salt in large bowl with electric mixer on medium speed until creamy. Add flour, ½ cup at a time, beating after each addition. Stir in dried fruit.

2 Shape dough into 14-inch log. Wrap in plastic wrap; refrigerate 1 hour.

3 Preheat oven to 300°F. Cut log into ½-inch slices; place on ungreased cookie sheets. Bake 20 to 25 minutes or until cookies are set and lightly browned. Cool on cookie sheets 5 minutes. Remove to wire racks; cool completely.

ONE-PAN
WONDERS

SEVEN-LAYER DESSERT

MAKES 2 TO 3 DOZEN BARS

½ cup (1 stick) butter, melted

1 teaspoon vanilla

1 cup graham cracker crumbs

1 cup butterscotch chips

1 cup chocolate chips

1 cup flaked coconut

1 cup chopped pecans, walnuts or almonds

1 can (14 ounces) sweetened condensed milk

1 Preheat oven to 350°F.

2 Pour butter into 13×9-inch baking dish. Add vanilla. Sprinkle cracker crumbs over butter. Layer butterscotch chips over crumbs, followed by chocolate chips, coconut and pecans. Pour sweetened condensed milk over mixture.

3 Bake 25 minutes or until lightly browned. Cool completely in pan. Cut into bars.

CRANBERRY-LIME DESSERT SQUARES

MAKES 2 TO 3 DOZEN BARS

2 cups all-purpose flour

½ cup powdered sugar, plus additional for dusting

1 tablespoon plus 1 teaspoon grated lime peel

¼ teaspoon plus ⅛ teaspoon salt, divided

1 cup (2 sticks) butter

2 cups granulated sugar

4 eggs

¼ cup cornstarch

1 teaspoon baking powder

¼ cup lime juice (about 2 limes)

1 cup dried cranberries

1 Preheat oven to 350°F. Grease 13×9-inch baking pan or line with parchment paper.

2 Combine flour, ½ cup powdered sugar, 1 tablespoon lime peel and ¼ teaspoon salt in medium bowl. Cut in butter with pastry blender or electric mixer on low speed until mixture forms coarse crumbs. Press mixture evenly into baking pan. Bake 18 to 20 minutes or until golden brown.

3 Combine granulated sugar and eggs in large bowl. Attach whisk attachment to stand mixer. Beat egg mixture on high speed 5 to 6 minutes or until thick, pale and triple in volume. Add cornstarch, lime juice, remaining 1 teaspoon lime peel, baking powder and remaining ⅛ teaspoon salt. Beat 3 to 5 minutes or until very well blended. Stir in cranberries. Pour over warm crust.

4 Bake about 25 minutes or until golden brown and set. Cool completely on wire rack. Sprinkle with additional powdered sugar. Refrigerate at least 2 hours. Cut into squares; serve cold. Store leftovers in refrigerator.

NOTE: If desired, tint lime filling with a few drops of food coloring.

SHORTBREAD TURTLE COOKIE BARS

MAKES 2 TO 3 DOZEN BARS

1¼ cups (2½ sticks) butter, softened, divided

1 cup all-purpose flour

1 cup old-fashioned oats

1¼ cups packed brown sugar, divided

½ teaspoon salt

½ teaspoon ground cinnamon

1½ cups chopped pecans

6 ounces bittersweet or semisweet chocolate, finely chopped

4 ounces white chocolate, finely chopped

1 Preheat oven to 350°F. Line 13×9-inch baking pan with foil or parchment paper or leave ungreased.

2 Beat ½ cup butter with electric mixer on medium speed 2 minutes or until light and fluffy. Add flour, oats, ¾ cup brown sugar, salt and cinnamon; beat on low speed until coarse crumbs form. Press firmly onto bottom of prepared pan.

3 Combine remaining ¾ cup butter and ¾ cup brown sugar in heavy medium saucepan. Cook over medium heat, stirring constantly until mixture comes to a boil. Boil 1 minute without stirring. Remove from heat; stir in pecans. Pour evenly over crust.

4 Bake 18 to 22 minutes or until caramel begins to bubble. Immediately sprinkle with bittersweet and white chocolates; swirl (do not spread) with knife after 45 seconds to 1 minute or when slightly softened. Cool completely in pan on wire rack. Cut into bars.

TOFFEE LATTE NUT BARS

MAKES 2 TO 3 DOZEN BARS

1½ cups all-purpose flour

¼ cup powdered sugar

½ teaspoon salt

¾ cup (1½ sticks) cold butter, cut into pieces

2 teaspoons instant coffee granules

1 teaspoon hot water

1 can (14 ounces) sweetened condensed milk

1 egg

1 teaspoon vanilla

1 package (8 ounces) toffee baking bits

1 cup chopped walnuts or pecans

¾ cup flaked coconut or 1 cup large coconut flakes

1 Preheat oven to 350°F. Line 13×9-inch pan with parchment paper or spray with nonstick cooking spray.

2 Combine flour, powdered sugar and salt in large bowl. Cut in butter with pastry blender or electric mixer on low speed until mixture resembles coarse crumbs. Press into prepared pan. Bake 15 minutes or until lightly browned around edges.

3 Meanwhile, dissolve coffee granules in hot water in small bowl. Pour sweetened condensed milk into medium bowl; whisk in coffee mixture. Whisk in egg and vanilla. Stir in toffee bits and walnuts. Pour over crust; sprinkle with coconut.

4 Bake 25 minutes or until filling is set and coconut is toasted. Cool 5 minutes, then loosen edges by running knife around sides of pan. Cool completely in pan on wire rack. Lift from pan using parchment; cut into bars.

CELEBRATION BROWNIES

MAKES 2 TO 3 DOZEN BROWNIES

1 cup (2 sticks) butter

8 ounces semisweet baking chocolate, coarsely chopped

1 cup sugar

4 eggs

1 teaspoon vanilla

1 teaspoon salt

1¼ cups all-purpose flour

2 cups dark or semisweet chocolate chips, divided

¼ cup whipping cream

1 container (about 2 ounces) rainbow nonpareils

1 Preheat oven to 350°F. Spray 13×9-inch baking pan with nonstick cooking spray or line with parchment paper.

2 Combine butter and chocolate in large heavy saucepan over low heat; stir until melted and well blended. Remove from heat; stir in sugar until blended. Stir in eggs, one at a time, until well blended after each addition. Stir in vanilla and salt. Add flour and 1 cup chocolate chips; stir just until blended. Spread batter evenly in prepared pan.

3 Bake 22 to 25 minutes or until center is set and toothpick inserted into center comes out clean. Cool completely in pan on wire rack.

4 Heat cream in small saucepan over medium-low heat until bubbles appear around edge of pan. Remove from heat; add remaining 1 cup chocolate chips. Let stand 1 minute; whisk until smooth and well blended. Spread evenly over top of brownies; sprinkle with nonpareils. Let stand until set. Cut into bars.

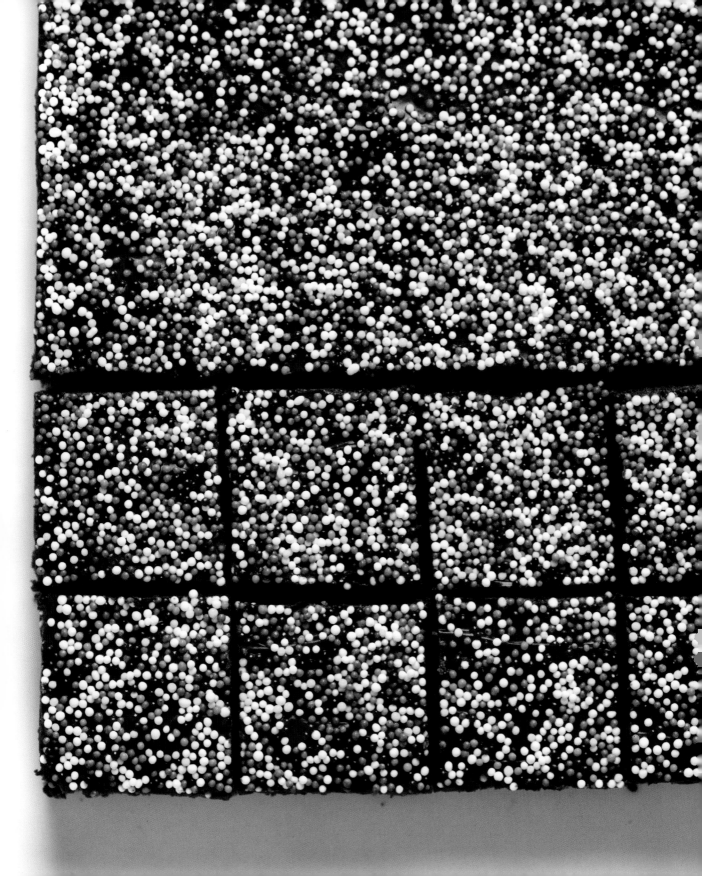

CHOCOLATE-TOPPED SHORTBREAD BARS

MAKES ABOUT 4½ DOZEN BARS

1½ cups packed brown sugar, divided

½ cup (1 stick) butter, softened

1 egg yolk

1 cup plus 2 tablespoons all-purpose flour, divided

2 eggs

1 cup semisweet chocolate chips

½ cup chopped toasted walnuts*

*To toast walnuts, spread in single layer on baking sheet. Bake in preheated 350°F oven 5 to 7 minutes or until golden brown, stirring frequently.

1 Preheat oven to 375°F. Spray 13×9-inch baking pan with nonstick cooking spray or line with parchment paper.

2 Beat ½ cup brown sugar, butter and egg yolk in large bowl with electric mixer on medium speed until light and smooth. Stir in 1 cup flour until well blended. Press dough onto bottom of prepared pan. Bake 12 to 15 minutes or until golden.

3 Meanwhile, beat remaining 1 cup brown sugar, 2 tablespoons flour and whole eggs in same bowl on medium speed until light and frothy. Spread mixture over partially baked crust.

4 Return to oven; bake about 15 minutes or until topping is set. Immediately sprinkle with chocolate chips. Let stand until chips melt, then spread chocolate evenly over bars. Sprinkle with walnuts. Cool completely in pan on wire rack. Cut into bars.

CHOCOLATE PEPPERMINT BARS

MAKES 16 BARS

CRUST

- 1 cup graham cracker crumbs
- 1 cup all-purpose flour
- ½ cup (1 stick) butter, melted
- ½ cup packed brown sugar
- ½ teaspoon baking powder

MINT LAYER

- 2¼ cups powdered sugar
- 3 tablespoons milk
- 1 tablespoon butter, melted
- 1 teaspoon peppermint extract

TOPPING

- 4 ounces bittersweet chocolate, melted

1 Preheat oven to 350°F. Line 9-inch square pan with foil.

2 Combine cracker crumbs, flour, ½ cup butter, brown sugar and baking powder in medium bowl; mix well. Press crumb mixture onto bottom of prepared pan.

3 Bake 20 minutes or until set. Cool completely in pan on wire rack.

4 Whisk powdered sugar, milk, 1 tablespoon butter and peppermint extract in medium bowl. Spread evenly onto cooled crust. Let stand 2 hours or until set.

5 Spread melted chocolate evenly over peppermint layer. Let stand until set. Cut into bars.

PUMPKIN STREUSEL BARS

MAKES 2 TO 3 DOZEN BARS

1½ cups all-purpose flour, divided

½ cup packed brown sugar

¼ cup (½ stick) butter, cut into small pieces

1 cup coarsely chopped pecans

1½ teaspoons baking powder

1 teaspoon ground cinnamon

¼ teaspoon salt

¼ teaspoon baking soda

⅛ teaspoon ground ginger

1 cup granulated sugar

1 cup canned pumpkin

½ cup vegetable oil

2 eggs

2 tablespoons butter, melted

1 Preheat oven to 350°F. Spray 13×9-inch baking pan with nonstick cooking spray or line with parchment paper.

2 For streusel, combine ½ cup flour and brown sugar in medium bowl. Cut in ¼ cup butter with pastry blender or electric mixer on low speed until mixture forms coarse crumbs. Stir in pecans.

3 Combine remaining 1 cup flour, baking powder, cinnamon, salt, baking soda and ginger in medium bowl; mix well.

4 Beat granulated sugar, pumpkin, oil, eggs and melted butter in large bowl with electric mixer on medium speed until well blended. Gradually add flour mixture; beat until blended. Spread batter in prepared pan; sprinkle with streusel.

5 Bake 35 minutes or until toothpick inserted into center comes out clean. Cool completely in pan on wire rack.

CHOCOLATE GINGERBREAD BROWNIES

MAKES 16 BROWNIES

BROWNIES

¾ cup all-purpose flour

½ cup unsweetened cocoa powder

2 teaspoons ground ginger

1 teaspoon ground cinnamon

½ teaspoon baking powder

½ teaspoon salt

⅛ teaspoon ground allspice

⅛ teaspoon ground cloves

⅛ teaspoon ground nutmeg

¾ cup granulated sugar

¾ cup packed brown sugar

¾ cup (1½ sticks) butter, melted and cooled

3 eggs

2 tablespoons molasses

1 teaspoon vanilla

FROSTING

¼ cup (½ stick) butter, melted

¼ cup buttermilk

½ teaspoon vanilla

2 cups powdered sugar

2 tablespoons unsweetened cocoa powder

1 teaspoon ground ginger

½ teaspoon ground cinnamon

1 Preheat oven to 350°F. Spray 8-inch square baking pan with nonstick cooking spray or line with parchment paper.

2 For brownies, whisk flour, ½ cup cocoa, 2 teaspoons ginger, 1 teaspoon cinnamon, baking powder, salt, allspice, cloves and nutmeg in large bowl. Whisk granulated sugar, brown sugar, ¾ cup butter, eggs, molasses and 1 teaspoon vanilla in medium bowl. Add to flour mixture; mix just until blended. Spread batter into prepared pan.

3 Bake 35 to 40 minutes or until toothpick inserted into center comes out clean. Cool completely in pan on wire rack.

4 For frosting, whisk ¼ cup butter, buttermilk and ½ teaspoon vanilla in small bowl. Add powdered sugar, 2 tablespoons cocoa, 1 teaspoon ginger and ½ teaspoon cinnamon; whisk until smooth. Spread evenly over brownies. Let stand until set. Cut into bars.

CARAMEL CHOCOLATE CHUNK BLONDIES

MAKES 2 TO 3 DOZEN BLONDIES

1½ cups all-purpose flour

1 teaspoon baking powder

1 teaspoon salt

¾ cup granulated sugar

¾ cup packed brown sugar

½ cup (1 stick) butter, softened

2 eggs

1½ teaspoons vanilla

1 package (11½ ounces) semisweet chocolate chunks *or* 10 ounces chopped bittersweet chocolate

5 tablespoons caramel ice cream topping

Flaky sea salt (optional)

1 Preheat oven to 350°F. Line 13×9-inch baking pan with parchment paper or spray with nonstick cooking spray.

2 Combine flour, baking powder and 1 teaspoon salt in medium bowl. Beat granulated sugar, brown sugar and butter in large bowl with electric mixer on medium speed until smooth and creamy. Beat in eggs and vanilla until well blended. Add flour mixture; beat on low speed until blended. Stir in chocolate chunks.

3 Spread batter evenly in prepared pan. Drop spoonfuls of caramel topping over batter; swirl into batter with knife. Sprinkle with sea salt, if desired.

4 Bake about 30 minutes or until edges are golden brown (center will be puffed and will not look set). Cool completely in pan on wire rack. Remove from pan using parchment; cut into bars.

BUTTERSCOTCH BROWNIES

MAKES 16 BROWNIES

1 cup butterscotch chips

½ cup packed brown sugar

¼ cup (½ stick) butter, softened

2 eggs

½ teaspoon vanilla

1 cup all-purpose flour

½ teaspoon baking powder

¼ teaspoon salt

1 cup semisweet chocolate chips

Unsweetened cocoa powder (optional)

1 Preheat oven to 350°F. Grease 9-inch square baking pan. Melt butterscotch chips in small saucepan over low heat, stirring constantly; set aside.

2 Beat brown sugar and butter in large bowl until light and fluffy. Beat in eggs, one at a time, scraping down side of bowl after each addition. Beat in melted butterscotch chips and vanilla. Combine flour, baking powder and salt in small bowl; add to butter mixture. Beat until well blended. Spread batter evenly in prepared pan.

3 Bake 20 to 25 minutes or until golden brown and center is set. Immediately sprinkle with chocolate chips. Let stand about 4 minutes or until chocolate is melted. Spread chocolate evenly over top. Cool completely in pan on wire rack. Sprinkle with cocoa, if desired. Cut into bars.

CHOCOLATE PECAN BARS

MAKES 2 TO 3 DOZEN BARS

CRUST

1⅓ cups all-purpose flour

½ cup (1 stick) butter, softened

¼ cup packed brown sugar

½ teaspoon salt

TOPPING

¾ cup light corn syrup

3 eggs, lightly beaten

2 tablespoons butter, melted and cooled

½ teaspoon vanilla

½ teaspoon almond extract

¾ cup milk chocolate chips

¾ cup semisweet chocolate chips

¾ cup chopped pecans, toasted*

¾ cup granulated sugar

To toast pecans, spread on baking sheet. Bake in preheated 350°F oven 5 to 7 minutes or until lightly browned and fragrant, stirring frequently.

1 Preheat oven to 350°F. Spray 13×9-inch baking pan with nonstick cooking spray.

2 For crust, combine flour, ½ cup butter, brown sugar and salt in medium bowl; mix with fork until crumbly. Press onto bottom of prepared baking pan. Bake 12 to 15 minutes or until lightly browned. Let stand 10 minutes.

3 Meanwhile, for topping, combine corn syrup, eggs, 2 tablespoons butter, vanilla and almond extract in large bowl; stir with fork until combined (do not beat). Fold in chocolate chips, pecans and granulated sugar until blended. Pour over baked crust.

4 Bake 25 to 30 minutes or until toothpick inserted into center comes out clean. Cool completely on wire rack. Cut into bars. Store in airtight container in refrigerator.

BUTTERSCOTCH TOFFEE GINGERSNAP SQUARES

MAKES 2 TO 3 DOZEN BARS

40 gingersnap cookies

6 tablespoons (¾ stick) butter, melted

1 cup butterscotch chips

½ cup pecan pieces

½ cup chopped peanuts

½ cup milk chocolate toffee bits

½ cup mini semisweet chocolate chips

1 can (14 ounces) sweetened condensed milk

1½ teaspoons vanilla

1 Preheat oven to 350°F. Line 13×9-inch baking pan with foil, leaving 1-inch overhang. Spray with nonstick cooking spray.

2 Place cookies in food processor; process until crumbs form. Measure 2 cups.

3 Combine 2 cups crumbs and butter in medium bowl; mix well. Press crumb mixture evenly onto bottom of prepared pan. Bake 4 to 5 minutes or until light brown around edges.

4 Meanwhile, combine butterscotch chips, pecans, peanuts, toffee bits and chocolate chips in medium bowl. Whisk sweetened condensed milk and vanilla in small bowl; pour over warm crust. Sprinkle with butterscotch mixture, pressing down gently.

5 Bake 15 to 18 minutes or until golden and bubbly. Cool completely in pan on wire rack. Remove foil; cut into bars.

DOUBLE CHOCOLATE DREAM BARS

MAKES 2 TO 3 DOZEN BARS

2¼ cups all-purpose flour, divided

1 cup (2 sticks) butter, softened

¾ cup powdered sugar, plus additional for garnish

⅓ cup unsweetened cocoa powder

½ teaspoon salt

2 cups granulated sugar

4 eggs, lightly beaten

4 ounces unsweetened baking chocolate, melted

1 Preheat oven to 350°F. Line 13×9-inch baking pan with parchment paper.

2 Beat 2 cups flour, butter, ¾ cup powdered sugar, cocoa and salt in large bowl with electric mixer on low speed until blended. Beat at medium speed until well blended and stiff dough forms. Press firmly onto bottom of prepared pan. Bake 15 to 20 minutes or just until set. *Do not overbake.*

3 Meanwhile, combine remaining ¼ cup flour and granulated sugar in large bowl. Stir in eggs and melted chocolate; beat with electric mixer on medium-high speed until well blended. Pour over crust.

4 Bake 25 minutes or until center is firm to the touch. Cool completely in pan on wire rack. Sprinkle with additional powdered sugar. Cut into bars.

COOKIE
PROJECTS

GINGERBREAD HOUSE

MAKES 2 HOUSES

1 cup (2 sticks) butter

1 cup packed brown sugar

1 cup molasses

1 egg

1 tablespoon ground ginger

1 teaspoon salt

1 teaspoon baking soda

1½ teaspoons ground cinnamon

1 teaspoon ground nutmeg

½ teaspoon ground allspice

5 cups all-purpose flour

Meringue Powder Royal Icing (page 134)

Assorted candies and decors (optional)

1 Copy house patterns on pages 135–137 at 100 percent; cut out and trace outlines onto cardboard. Cut out patterns and label them.

2 Beat butter and brown sugar in large bowl with electric mixer on medium speed until light and fluffy. Beat in molasses and egg until well blended; scrape down side of bowl. Stir in ginger, salt, baking soda, cinnamon, nutmeg and allspice. Add flour; beat on low speed until stiff dough forms. Shape dough into two discs; wrap in plastic wrap and refrigerate 1 hour or until firm.

3 Preheat oven to 375°F. Line two large cookie sheets with parchment paper. Roll out dough on floured surface with floured rolling pin ¼ inch thick. Place patterns on dough; cut four of each. Cut windows and door from front pieces with paring knife. Cut windows as desired from remaining side and back pieces.

4 Bake 8 minutes. Remove from oven; carefully trim about 1⁄16 inch off of each edge. Bake 5 to 8 minutes or until lightly browned and firm. Cool on cookie sheets 3 minutes. Carefully transfer to wire racks with large spatula; cool completely.

5 To make base of house, cover 12-inch-square piece of heavy cardboard with parchment paper or decorative paper. Prepare Meringue Powder Royal Icing.

6 Spoon icing into piping bag fitted with writing tip or resealable freezer bag with one small corner cut off. Decorate house as desired; let stand until icing is set.

7 Pipe icing on edges of all pieces. Glue cookies together, two pieces at a time, at seams and onto base. Prop up house pieces with cans until icing is set before attaching additional pieces. Pipe icing along each edge to reinforce roof and walls. Let stand 1 hour or until set.

MERINGUE POWDER ROYAL ICING

MAKES ABOUT 2½ CUPS

¼ cup plus 2 tablespoons water

¼ cup meringue powder*

1 package (16 ounces) powdered sugar, sifted

Available online and where cake decorating supplies are sold.

1 Beat water and meringue powder in medium bowl with electric mixer on low speed until well blended. Beat on high speed about 5 minutes or until stiff peaks form.

2 Beat in powdered sugar on low speed until well blended. Beat on high speed until icing is very stiff. Cover icing with damp cloth to prevent it from drying out.

NOTE: This icing is very stiff and will harden after 5 minutes, and it completely dries in 20 to 30 minutes. To decorate cutout cookies, thin icing with additional water until desired piping or spreading consistency is reached.

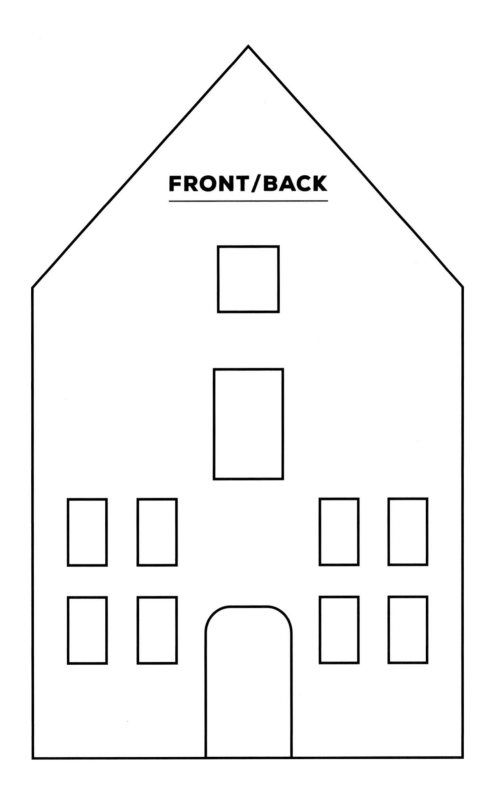

FRONT/BACK

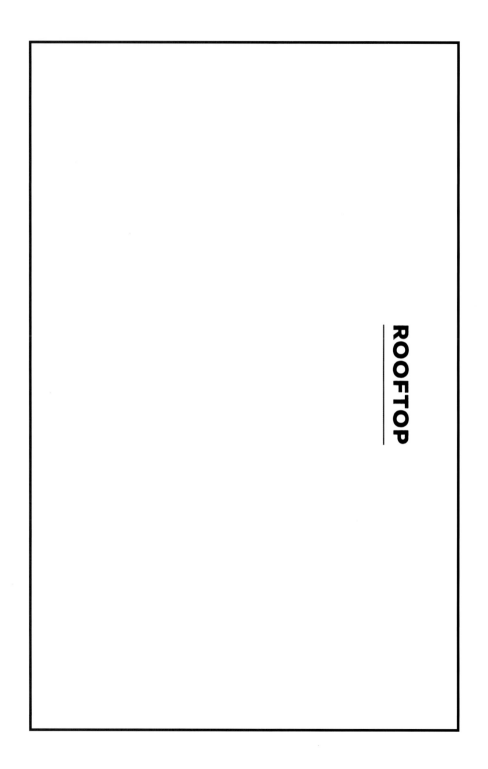

ROOFTOP

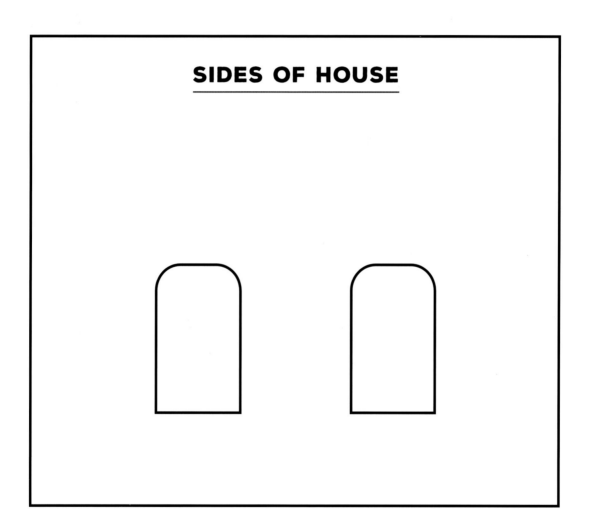

SIDES OF HOUSE

SPARKLING SNOWFLAKES

MAKES 1½ TO 2 DOZEN COOKIES

1¾ cups all-purpose flour

1 teaspoon baking powder

⅛ teaspoon salt

½ cup granulated sugar

¼ cup (½ stick) butter, softened

1 egg

Grated peel of 1 lemon

White Icing (recipe follows)*

Decorating sugar, edible glitter and decors (optional)

To make blue icing, add blue food coloring, a few drops at a time, until desired shade is reached.

1 Combine flour, baking powder and salt in medium bowl. Beat granulated sugar and butter in large bowl with electric mixer on medium speed until well blended. Add egg and lemon peel; beat until well blended. Gradually add flour mixture on low speed. (Dough will be sticky.) Shape dough into a disc; wrap tightly in plastic wrap. Refrigerate 2 to 3 hours or until firm.

2 Preheat oven to 375°F. Line cookie sheets with parchment paper. Roll dough between floured sheets of parchment paper to ¼-inch thickness. Remove top sheet of parchment; cut out shapes with floured 2½- to 5-inch snowflake cookie cutters. Place cutouts on prepared cookie sheets. Repeat with trimmings.

3 Bake 8 to 10 minutes or until set but not browned. Cool on cookie sheets 1 minute. Remove to wire racks; cool completely.

4 Prepare White Icing; tint some of icing blue, if desired. Spread or pipe icing onto cookies; decorate as desired. Let cookies stand until icing is set.

WHITE ICING: Beat 4 cups powdered sugar, ¼ cup water and 3 tablespoons meringue powder in large bowl with electric mixer on high speed 6 to 7 minutes or until icing is of spreading consistency.

STAINED GLASS COOKIES

MAKES ABOUT 2 DOZEN COOKIES

¾ cup (1½ sticks) butter, softened

¾ cup sugar

3 egg yolks

1 teaspoon vanilla

2 cups all-purpose flour

¼ teaspoon salt

Multi-colored hard candies

Meringue Powder Royal Icing (page 134) or White Icing (page 138)

Edible glitter or coarse sugar

SUPPLIES

Plastic straw

Various ribbons

1 Beat butter and sugar in large bowl with electric mixer at medium speed 1 minute. Beat in egg yolks and vanilla until well blended. Add flour and salt; beat just until combined. Shape dough into 2 discs. Wrap each disc in plastic wrap. Refrigerate dough at least 2 hours or overnight.

2 Meanwhile, separate candies by color. Place into small resealable freezer bags; seal bags. Using a heavy object, such as a meat mallet or small saucepan, crush candies. Set aside.

3 Preheat oven to 350°F. Line cookie sheets with parchment paper. On lightly floured surface, roll out dough to ¼-inch thickness for smaller cookies. For cookies over 4 inches in diameter, roll out dough to ½-inch thickness. Cut into desired shapes; place 2 inches apart on prepared sheets. Re-roll dough scraps once.

4 Create small cut outs in cookies using mini cookie cutters. Remove dough from small cut outs and discard. Fill cut outs with selected colors of crushed candies.

5 Bake 12 to 15 minutes until cookies are lightly browned and sugars are melted. (Larger cookies may take longer to bake.) Cool cookies on cookie sheets 5 minutes. Carefully remove to wire racks; cool completely.

6 Prepare icing; thin with enough water to spreadable consistency. Spread or pipe icing on cookies. Sprinkle with glitter before icing sets. Let iced cookies dry completely before serving or hanging. Store in airtight container.

VARIATION: To hang cookies as ornaments, punch out small hole with plastic straw at top of cookie about ½-inch from edge after placing desired shapes onto baking sheets.

RAINBOWS

MAKES ABOUT 5 DOZEN COOKIES

2¼ cups all-purpose flour

¼ teaspoon salt

1 cup sugar

¾ cup (1½ sticks) butter, softened

1 egg

1 teaspoon vanilla

1 teaspoon almond extract

Red, green, yellow and blue paste food coloring

White frosting and edible gold glitter

1 Combine flour and salt in medium bowl. Beat sugar and butter in large bowl with electric mixer on medium speed until fluffy. Beat in egg, vanilla and almond extract. Gradually add flour mixture. Beat on low speed until well blended. Divide dough into 10 equal pieces. Combine 4 sections of dough and red food coloring in large bowl; blend until smooth.

2 Combine 3 pieces of dough and green food coloring in medium bowl; blend until smooth.

3 Combine 2 pieces of dough and yellow food coloring in another medium bowl; blend until smooth.

4 Combine remaining dough and blue food coloring in small bowl; blend until smooth. Wrap each section of dough in plastic wrap. Refrigerate 30 minutes.

5 Shape blue dough into 8-inch log. Shape yellow dough into 8×3-inch rectangle; place on waxed paper. Place blue log in center of yellow rectangle. Fold yellow edges up and around blue log, pinching to seal. Roll to form smooth log.

6 Roll green dough into 8×5-inch rectangle on waxed paper. Place yellow log in center of green rectangle. Fold green edges up and around yellow log. Pinch to seal. Roll gently to form smooth log.

7 Roll red dough into 8×7-inch rectangle. Place green log in center of red rectangle. Fold red edges up and around green log. Pinch to seal. Roll gently to form smooth log. Wrap in plastic wrap. Refrigerate 1 hour.

8 Preheat oven to 350°F. Line cookie sheets with parchment paper. Cut log in half lengthwise. Cut each half into ¼-inch-thick slices. Place slices 1 inch apart on prepared cookie sheets. Bake 8 to 12 minutes or until set but not browned. Cool on cookie sheets 1 minute. Remove to wire racks; cool completely.

9 Pipe small amount of frosting on bottom corner of one side of each cookie and sprinkle with glitter. Let stand 1 hour or until frosting sets.

CANDY WREATH ORNAMENTS

MAKES ABOUT 2 DOZEN COOKIES

1 cup (2 sticks) butter, softened

½ cup powdered sugar

2 tablespoons packed brown sugar

¼ teaspoon salt

1 egg

1 teaspoon vanilla

2 cups all-purpose flour

4 to 5 drops green food coloring

Mini candy-coated chocolate pieces

1 Beat butter, powdered sugar, brown sugar and salt in large bowl with electric mixer on medium speed 2 minutes or until light and fluffy. Add egg and vanilla; beat until well blended. Gradually add flour on low speed until blended. Divide dough in half; set one half aside. Add green color to remaining dough; beat until blended. Shape both doughs into discs; wrap in plastic wrap and refrigerate 1 hour.

2 Preheat oven to 300°F. Shape green dough into 28 (5-inch) ropes. Repeat with plain dough. For each wreath, twist 1 green and 1 plain rope together, pressing ends together. Place on ungreased cookie sheets. Press candies onto wreaths.

3 Bake 15 to 18 minutes or until lightly browned. Cool on cookie sheets 5 minutes. Remove to wire racks; cool completely.

HOLIDAY COOKIE TREE

MAKES 1 TREE

5 cups all-purpose flour

6 teaspoons pumpkin pie spice

1 teaspoon baking soda

1 teaspoon salt

1¼ cups molasses

1 cup sugar

1 cup shortening or butter, melted and cooled slightly

3 eggs

Green food coloring

Meringue Powder Royal Icing (page 134) or White Icing (page 138)

Multicolored round decors

Powdered sugar (optional)

SUPPLIES

Holiday cookie tree cutter set

1 Combine flour, pumpkin pie spice, baking soda and salt in large bowl. Beat molasses, sugar, shortening and eggs in large bowl with electric mixer on medium speed. Gradually add flour mixture on low speed until blended. Divide dough in half; shape each half into a disc. Refrigerate at least 1 hour or overnight.

2 Preheat oven to 350°F. Line cookie sheets with parchment paper. Roll out dough to ¼-inch thickness on lightly floured surface.

3 Using holiday tree cookie cutter set, cut 2 of each star, grouping large stars together, medium stars together and small stars together.

4 Bake large stars 10 to 15 minutes, medium stars 6 to 10 minutes and small stars 4 to 5 minutes or until lightly browned on edges. Cool on cookie sheets 2 minutes. Remove to wire racks; cool completely.

5 Prepare icing; tint desired shade of green, or leave white. Place in piping bag fitted with medium writing tip.

6 Stack cookies, largest to smallest, alternating tips and using dab of icing to adhere layers. Pip icing in zigzag on each star tip for branches. Pipe frosting on top cookie for top of tree. Decorate with decors for ornaments before icing sets. Sprinkle with powdered sugar, if desired.

PINWHEEL COOKIES

MAKES 4 DOZEN COOKIES

½ cup (1 stick) butter, softened

1 package (8 ounces) cream cheese, softened

3 cups all-purpose flour

¼ teaspoon salt

Powdered sugar

½ cup seedless raspberry jam

1 Preheat oven to 350°F. Grease cookie sheets or line with parchment paper.

2 Beat butter and cream cheese in large bowl with electric mixer on medium speed 2 minutes or until well blended. Combine flour and salt in small bowl. Gradually add to cream cheese mixture, beating until well blended. Divide dough in half; shape each half into A rectangle. Wrap dough in plastic wrap; refrigerate at least 30 minutes.

3 Dust work surface with powdered sugar; roll out 1 dough piece into 15-inch square. Trim and cut into 3-inch squares. Slice squares from each corner. Fold half of each corner towards center. Place on prepared cookie sheets. Repeat with remaining dough.

4 Bake 20 to 25 minutes. Remove from oven; spoon ½ teaspoon jam onto center of each cookie. Bake 5 to 10 minutes or until golden brown. Remove to wire racks; cool completely. Dust with powdered sugar, if desired.

VARIATION: Use a mixture of cinnamon and granulated sugar instead of the powdered sugar. Sprinkle jam centers with finely chopped pecans before baking.

CHRISTMAS STOCKING COOKIES

MAKES ABOUT 1 DOZEN COOKIES

5 cups all-purpose flour

1 tablespoon ground ginger

2 teaspoons ground cinnamon

1 teaspoon salt

1 cup granulated sugar

1 cup shortening or butter

1 cup molasses

Meringue Powder Royal Icing (page 134) or White Icing (page 138)

Red and green food colorings

Assorted decors

White nonpareils

Edible food color markers

SUPPLIES

Large stocking cookie cutter

Plastic straw

Various ribbons

1 Preheat oven to 350°F. Line cookie sheets with parchment paper. Sift together flour, ginger, cinnamon and salt in medium bowl.

2 Combine granulated sugar, shortening and molasses in medium saucepan. Stir over low heat just until shortening melts. Pour into large mixing bowl. Let cool 5 minutes.

3 Add flour mixture to warm sugar mixture. Beat with electric mixer on low speed just until dough forms, adding additional flour if needed to form soft but not sticky dough. Let dough rest 5 minutes.

4 Roll warm dough on lightly floured surface ½-inch thick. Cut out stockings using a cutter or stencil. Re-roll dough scraps once. Place cookies 2 inches apart on prepared cookie sheets. Using plastic straw, punch holes at top corner of stockings about ½-inch from edge. Bake 18 to 20 minutes or until cookies are golden brown. Cool on cookie sheets 5 minutes. Remove to wire racks; cool completely.

5 Prepare icing. Tint some of icing green and/or red; thin with water to desired spreading consistency. Spread or pipe icing over cookies. Pipe or spread white frosting at tops, toes and heels of cookies. Decorate with decors before icing hardens. Re-punch plastic straw into hole to remove icing before it sets. Let stand until icing is completely hardened. Write names on tops of cookies with edible markers.

6 To hang cookies, cut pieces of ribbon to desired length. Slip ribbon through hole and make a small knot.

NOTE: This recipe produces a very firm and crunchy cookie. For decorative gingerbread pieces, such as gingerbread houses and hanging cookies, use recipes without eggs and leavening for an even firmer cookie. Eliminating the eggs also keeps the finished cut outs from spreading.

COZY FIRES

½ cup (1 stick) butter, softened

¾ cup sugar

1 egg

1 teaspoon vanilla

½ teaspoon salt

1½ cups all-purpose flour

½ cup unsweetened cocoa powder

2 cups broken thin pretzel sticks

1 tube (4¼ ounces) yellow star icing with decorating tip

1 tube (4¼ ounces) orange star icing with decorating tip

1 Beat butter and sugar in large bowl with electric mixer on medium speed until light and fluffy. Add egg, vanilla and salt; beat until well blended. Add flour and cocoa; beat on low speed just until blended. Shape dough into a ball; wrap in plastic wrap and refrigerate 1 hour or until firm.

2 Preheat oven to 350°F. Line cookie sheets with parchment paper. Shape dough into ½-inch balls. Place 2 inches apart on prepared cookie sheets.

3 Bake 12 minutes or until puffed and nearly set. Immediately press pretzel pieces into sides of cookies to resemble logs. Remove to wire racks; cool completely.

4 Using decorating tips, pipe yellow and orange icing onto cooled cookies to resemble flames.

CHOCOLATE COOKIE POPS

MAKES 16 COOKIES

COOKIE POPS

- 2 cups all-purpose flour
- ½ cup unsweetened cocoa powder
- ½ teaspoon baking powder
- ½ teaspoon salt
- 1 cup (2 sticks) butter, softened
- 1 cup granulated sugar
- ½ cup packed brown sugar
- 1 egg
- 1 teaspoon vanilla

GLAZES

- ½ cup white chocolate chips or chopped white chocolate candy bar
- ½ cup semisweet chocolate chips
- 1 teaspoon shortening, divided

  Sprinkles and/or decors

SUPPLIES

  Decorative paper straws

1 Preheat oven to 350°F. Line cookie sheets with parchment paper.

2 Combine flour, cocoa, baking powder and salt in medium bowl. Beat butter, granulated sugar and brown sugar in large bowl with electric mixer on medium-high speed until light and fluffy. Beat in egg and vanilla until well blended. Gradually beat in flour mixture on low speed.

3 Roll scant ¼ cupfuls (2 ounces) of dough into balls; place 3 inches apart on prepared cookie sheets. Flatten dough until 2 inches in diameter.

4 Bake 14 to 16 minutes or until cookies are set. Immediately remove to wire racks. Carefully insert straws into hot cookies all the way to top. If needed, trim uneven crispy edges from cookies with sharp knife. Cool completely.

5 For icing, melt semisweet chocolate chips and ½ teaspoon shortening in small bowl. Microwave on HIGH 30 seconds or until melted and smooth. Repeat with white chocolate chips and remaining ½ teaspoon shortening. Place glazes in separate small resealable food storage bags with small corners cut off. Pipe in spiral shape on cookies; immediately sprinkle with decors.

YULE TREE NAMESAKES

MAKES 2 DOZEN PLACE CARDS

COOKIES

¾ cup (1½ sticks) butter, softened

¼ cup granulated sugar

¼ cup packed brown sugar

1 egg yolk

1¾ cups all-purpose flour

¾ teaspoon baking powder

¼ teaspoon salt

GLAZE AND GARNISHES

4 cups plus 1 to 2 tablespoons powdered sugar, divided

4 to 6 tablespoons milk

Green food coloring

Assorted candies

3 packages (12 ounces each) semisweet chocolate chips, melted

1 cup flaked coconut, tinted green*

To tint coconut, combine small amount of food coloring (paste or liquid) with 1 teaspoon water in large bowl. Add coconut and stir until evenly coated. Add more coloring, if needed.

1 For cookies, beat butter, granulated sugar, brown sugar and egg yolk in large bowl; beat on medium speed until blended. Add flour, baking powder and salt; mix well. Cover and refrigerate until firm, about 4 hours or overnight.

2 Preheat oven to 350°F. Roll out dough on floured surface to ⅛-inch thickness. Cut out cookies using 3- to 4-inch tree-shaped cookie cutter. Place 2 inches apart on ungreased cookie sheets.

3 Bake 9 to 11 minutes until edges begin to brown. Remove to wire racks; cool completely.

4 For glaze, combine 4 cups powdered sugar and enough milk to make a medium-thick pourable glaze. Reserve ⅓ cup glaze; tint remaining glaze green with food coloring. Place cookies on wire rack set over waxed paper-lined cookie sheet. Spoon green glaze over cookies.

5 Add remaining 1 to 2 tablespoons powdered sugar to reserved glaze until glaze is stiff enough to pipe. Spoon into pastry bag fitted with small writing tip. Pipe names onto trees. Decorate with candies as desired. Let cookies stand until set.

6 Line 24 mini (1¾-inch) muffin cups with foil baking cups. Spoon melted chocolate into prepared muffin cups, filling evenly. Let stand until chocolate is very thick and partially set. Place trees upright in chocolate. Sprinkle tinted coconut over chocolate. Let stand until set.

CHRISTMAS LIGHTS AND ORNAMENT COOKIES

MAKES 2 DOZEN COOKIES

¾ cup (1½ sticks) butter, softened

¾ cup sugar

3 egg yolks

1 teaspoon vanilla

2 cups all-purpose flour

¼ teaspoon salt

White Icing (page 138)

Food coloring

Decors, colored sugars and edible glitters

SUPPLIES

Ornament cookie cutters

Plastic straw

Various ribbons

1 Beat butter and sugar in large bowl with electric mixer on medium speed 1 minute. Beat in egg yolks and vanilla until well blended. Add flour and salt; beat just until combined. Divide dough in half; shape each half into a disc and wrap in plastic wrap. Refrigerate at least 2 hours or overnight.

2 Preheat oven to 350°F. Line cookie sheets with parchment paper.

3 Roll out dough ¼-inch thick on lightly floured surface. Cut out ornaments and lights with cutters or stencils. Re-roll dough scraps once. Place cutouts on prepared cookie sheets 1 inch apart. Using plastic straw, punch hole at the top of each cookie, about ¼-inch from edge.

4 Bake 12 to 15 minutes or until golden brown. Cool cookies on cookie sheets 5 minutes. Remove to wire racks; cool completely.

5 Prepare icing. Thin with water to soft, spreadable consistency. Divide icing into as many small bowls as desired colors. Keep all icings covered with damp paper towels. Pipe or spread icing over cookies. Sprinkle with sugars or decors before icing hardens.

6 To hang cookies, cut pieces of ribbon to desired length. Slip ribbon through hole and make a small knot.

GIFTABLE
SWEETS

CANDY CANE FUDGE

MAKES ABOUT 2 POUNDS (64 PIECES)

½ cup light corn syrup

½ cup whipping cream

3 cups semisweet chocolate chips

1½ cups powdered sugar, sifted

1¼ cups crushed candy canes, divided

1½ teaspoons vanilla

1 Line 8-inch baking pan with foil, leaving 1-inch overhang on sides.

2 Bring corn syrup and cream to a boil in 2-quart saucepan over medium heat. Boil 1 minute. Remove from heat. Add chocolate chips; stir constantly until chips are melted. Stir in powdered sugar, 1 cup candy canes and vanilla. Pour into prepared pan. Sprinkle with remaining ¼ cup candy canes. Cover and refrigerate 2 hours or until firm.

3 Lift fudge out of pan using foil. Place on cutting board; remove foil. Cut into 1-inch squares. Store in airtight container.

WINTRY WHITE CHOCOLATE BARK

MAKES ABOUT 2 POUNDS

1½ pounds white chocolate, coarsely chopped

1 cup pistachios, toasted*

½ cup dried cherries

½ cup dried cranberries

*To toast pistachios, spread in single layer in heavy skillet. Cook over medium heat 1 to 2 minutes or until nuts are lightly browned, stirring frequently. Remove from skillet immediately. Cool before using.

1 Line large cookie sheet with parchment paper or waxed paper.

2 Melt chocolate in top of double boiler over simmering water, stirring occasionally until melted. Remove from heat. Add pistachios, cherries and cranberries; stir until evenly coated. Pour onto center of prepared cookie sheet. Spread to ½- to ⅜-inch thickness using knife or offset spatula. Let stand several hours or overnight to cool completely. (Do not refrigerate.)

3 Cut or break into pieces.

CITRUS CANDIED NUTS

MAKES ABOUT 3 CUPS

1 egg white

1½ cups whole almonds

1½ cups pecan halves

1 cup powdered sugar

2 tablespoons lemon juice

2 teaspoons grated orange peel

1 teaspoon grated lemon peel

½ teaspoon salt

⅛ teaspoon ground nutmeg

1 Preheat oven to 300°F. Grease 15×10-inch baking pan.

2 Beat egg white in medium bowl with electric mixer on high speed until soft peaks form. Add almonds and pecans; stir until well coated. Stir in powdered sugar, lemon juice, orange peel, lemon peel, salt and nutmeg until evenly coated. Spread nuts in single layer in prepared pan.

3 Bake 30 minutes, stirring after 20 minutes. Turn off heat. Let nuts stand in oven 15 minutes. Remove nuts from pan to sheet of foil. Cool completely. Store in airtight container up to 2 weeks.

CLASSIC ENGLISH TOFFEE

MAKES ABOUT 1¼ POUNDS TOFFEE

1 cup (2 sticks) butter

1 cup sugar

2 tablespoons water

¼ teaspoon salt

1 teaspoon vanilla

3 ounces semisweet chocolate, chopped

3 ounces bittersweet chocolate, chopped

½ cup chopped toasted pecans*

*To toast pecans, spread in single layer in heavy skillet. Cook and stir over medium heat 1 to 2 minutes or until nuts are lightly browned, stirring frequently.

1 Line 9-inch square pan with heavy-duty foil, leaving 1-inch overhang on all sides.

2 Combine butter, sugar, water and salt in heavy 2- or 2½-quart saucepan. Bring to a boil over medium heat, stirring frequently. Attach candy thermometer to side of pan. Continue boiling about 20 minutes or until sugar mixture reaches hard-crack stage (305° to 310°F), stirring frequently. Watch closely after temperature reaches 290°F. Temperature will rise quickly and mixture will burn above 310°F. Remove from heat; stir in vanilla. Immediately pour into prepared pan, spreading to edges. Cool completely.

3 Microwave chocolates in small microwavable bowl on MEDIUM (50%) 3 to 4 minutes or until melted, stirring every minute.

4 Spread chocolate evenly over toffee; sprinkle with pecans. Refrigerate about 30 minutes or until chocolate is set.

5 Carefully break toffee into pieces without dislodging pecans. Store in airtight container at room temperature between sheets of waxed paper.

BUTTERSCOTCH-CHOCOLATE DIVINITY

MAKES ABOUT 3 DOZEN PIECES

2 cups sugar

⅓ cup light corn syrup

⅓ cup water

2 egg whites

⅛ teaspoon cream of tartar

1 teaspoon vanilla

½ cup milk chocolate chips

½ cup butterscotch chips

½ cup chopped pecans or walnuts

1 Line two baking sheets with parchment paper.

2 Combine sugar, corn syrup and water in medium heavy saucepan. Cook over medium heat without stirring until sugar dissolves and mixture comes to a boil. Clip candy thermometer to side of pan, making sure bulb is submerged in sugar mixture but not touching bottom of pan. Continue to cook until mixture reaches the hard-ball stage (255°F).

3 Meanwhile, beat egg whites and cream of tartar in large bowl with electric mixer on high speed until stiff but not dry. With mixer running on high speed, slowly pour hot syrup into egg whites in thin steady stream. Add vanilla; beat until candy forms soft peaks and starts to lose its gloss. Stir in chocolate chips, butterscotch chips and nuts with spatula.

4 Working quickly, drop mixture by tablespoonfuls with spoon or small cookie scoop onto prepared baking sheets. Store in refrigerator in airtight container between layers of waxed paper or freeze up to 3 months.

CHOCOLATE PEANUT CRUNCH

MAKES ABOUT ¾ POUND

1 cup milk chocolate chips

½ cup semisweet chocolate chips

2 tablespoons light corn syrup

1 tablespoon shortening

½ cup roasted peanuts

2 teaspoons vanilla

1 Butter 8-inch square baking pan.

2 Melt milk and semisweet chocolate chips with corn syrup and shortening in small heavy saucepan over low heat, stirring constantly.

3 Stir in peanuts and vanilla. Spread in prepared pan, distributing peanuts evenly. Refrigerate until firm. Break into pieces.

MOCHA FUDGE

MAKES ABOUT 1¾ POUNDS

1¾ cups sugar

¾ cup whipping cream

1 tablespoon instant coffee granules

1 tablespoon light corn syrup

1 cup milk chocolate chips

1 cup (half of 7-ounce jar) marshmallow creme

½ cup chopped walnuts or pecans

1 teaspoon vanilla

1 Butter 8-inch square pan. Lightly butter side of medium heavy saucepan.

2 Combine sugar, cream, coffee granules and corn syrup in prepared saucepan. Cook over medium heat until sugar is dissolved and mixture comes to a boil, stirring constantly. Wash down side of saucepan with pastry brush frequently dipped in hot water to remove sugar crystals. Boil 5 minutes.

3 Meanwhile, combine chocolate chips, marshmallow creme, nuts and vanilla in heatproof bowl.

4 Pour sugar mixture over chocolate mixture; stir until chips are melted. Spread evenly in prepared pan. Score fudge into squares with knife. Refrigerate until firm.

5 Cut into squares along score lines. Store covered in refrigerator.

PISTACHIO-ORANGE BISCOTTI

MAKES 40 BISCOTTI

1½ cups all-purpose flour

1 cup whole wheat flour

¼ teaspoon baking soda

¼ teaspoon salt

⅔ cup sugar

½ cup canola oil

2 eggs

2 teaspoons vanilla

2 teaspoons grated orange peel

½ cup coarsely chopped pistachios

1 Preheat oven to 350°F. Combine all-purpose flour, whole wheat flour, baking soda and salt in medium bowl.

2 Beat sugar, oil, eggs, vanilla and orange peel in large bowl with spoon until blended. Stir in flour mixture; add nuts.

3 Place dough on lightly floured surface. Knead 15 times until smooth. Divide dough in half; shape each half into 10×3-inch rectangle. Place on ungreased cookie sheet.

4 Bake 25 to 30 minutes or until toothpick inserted into center comes out clean. Cool on cookie sheet 15 minutes. Cut each rectangle crosswise into ½-inch slices. Place slices, cut side down, on cookie sheet.

5 Bake 15 to 18 minutes longer or until light brown, turning once. (Biscotti will crisp as they cool.) Remove to wire rack; cool completely.

TOFFEE CHOCOLATE CRISPIES

MAKES ABOUT 2 DOZEN CANDIES

1 cup slivered almonds

1 cup crisp rice cereal

½ cup milk chocolate toffee bits

1 cup milk or semisweet chocolate chips

1 teaspoon shortening

1 Line baking sheet or large tray with foil. Place almonds in medium nonstick skillet; toast over medium heat 7 to 8 minutes or until lightly browned, stirring frequently. Place almonds in large bowl; stir in cereal and toffee bits.

2 Place chocolate chips and shortening in medium microwavable bowl. Microwave on HIGH 30 seconds; stir. Microwave at 10-second intervals; stir until melted and smooth. Pour chocolate mixture over almond mixture; stir until evenly coated.

3 Drop mixture by rounded tablespoonfuls onto prepared baking sheet. Refrigerate 30 minutes or until cool and solid. Serve immediately or store between layers of waxed paper in airtight container in refrigerator up to 1 week.

CLASSIC RUM BALLS

MAKES 4 TO 5 DOZEN CANDIES

2 cups vanilla cookie crumbs (about 60 vanilla wafers)

2 tablespoons unsweetened cocoa powder

2 cups powdered sugar, divided

1 cup finely chopped walnuts or pecans

¼ teaspoon salt

½ cup light corn syrup

1 tablespoon honey

2 teaspoons rum extract

½ teaspoon vanilla

1 Combine cookie crumbs, cocoa, 1 cup powdered sugar, walnuts and salt in large bowl; stir well.

2 Add corn syrup, honey, rum extract and vanilla. Knead until mixture comes together. Shape into 1-inch balls.

3 Place remaining 1 cup powdered sugar in medium bowl; roll balls in sugar to coat.

TIP: To make cookie crumbs, place cookies in food processor or blender, and process until finely ground. Or place cookies in large resealable food storage bag, and use rolling pin to crush cookies into fine crumbs.

VARIATION: Substitute 1 teaspoon orange juice for the rum and increase the vanilla to 1 teaspoon.

FUDGY MARSHMALLOW POPCORN

MAKES ABOUT 4 QUARTS

3½ quarts popped popcorn
(about 14 cups)

2 cups sugar

1 cup evaporated milk

¼ cup (½ stick) butter

1 cup (½ of 7-ounce jar)
marshmallow creme

1 cup semisweet chocolate
chips

1 teaspoon vanilla

1 Spray baking sheets with nonstick cooking spray
or line with parchment paper. Place popcorn in
large bowl.

2 Combine sugar, evaporated milk and butter in
medium saucepan. Cook over medium heat until
sugar is dissolved and mixture comes to a boil,
stirring constantly. Boil 5 minutes. Remove from
heat. Stir in marshmallow creme, chocolate chips
and vanilla until chocolate is melted and mixture
is smooth.

3 Pour chocolate mixture over popcorn, stirring
until completely coated. Spread in single layer on
prepared baking sheets. Refrigerate until set.

HINT: Remove any unpopped kernels before
measuring the popped popcorn.

NUTTY COOKIE BALLS

MAKES 2 TO 3 DOZEN CANDIES

1½ cups butter cookie crumbs
   (about 22 butter cookies)

1 cup chopped honey-roasted
   peanuts

½ cup chopped golden raisins*

½ cup flaked coconut

⅓ cup light corn syrup

2 tablespoons honey

2 tablespoons smooth or
   crunchy peanut butter

⅓ cup unsweetened cocoa
   powder

*Spray knife with nonstick cooking
spray to prevent sticking.

1 Combine cookie crumbs, peanuts, raisins and coconut in large bowl; stir well.

2 Add corn syrup, honey and peanut butter. Knead by hand until mixture comes together. Shape into 1-inch balls.

3 Spread cocoa on baking sheet; roll balls in cocoa to coat.

VARIATION: If desired, roll balls in finely ground peanuts, powdered sugar, flaked coconut or melted chocolate.

TIP: To make cookie crumbs, place cookies in food processor or blender; process until finely ground. Or place in large resealable food storage bag, and use rolling pin to crush into fine crumbs.

CHOCOLATE PEPPERMINTS

MAKES ABOUT 100 CANDIES

1 cup semisweet chocolate chips

1 cup milk chocolate chips

¼ teaspoon peppermint extract

½ cup crushed peppermint candy

1 Line baking sheet with buttered waxed paper.

2 Melt chips in heavy medium saucepan over very low heat, stirring constantly. Stir in peppermint extract. Spread mixture in rectangle about ¼ inch thick on prepared baking sheet. Sprinkle with candy; press into chocolate. Refrigerate until almost firm.

3 Cut into 1-inch squares. Refrigerate until firm before removing from paper.

TIP: Squares are easier to cut without breaking if chocolate is not completely firm.

BUTTER COOKIES

MAKES ABOUT 2 DOZEN COOKIES

¾ cup (1½ sticks) butter, softened

¼ cup granulated sugar

¼ cup packed brown sugar

1 egg yolk

1¾ cups all-purpose flour

¾ teaspoon baking powder

⅛ teaspoon salt

1 Beat butter, sugars and egg yolk in medium bowl until well blended. Add flour, baking powder and salt; beat until well blended. Cover; refrigerate until firm, about 4 hours or overnight.

2 Preheat oven to 350°F. Roll out dough on lightly floured surface ¼-inch thick. Cut into desired shapes with 1-inch cookie cutters. Place cutouts on ungreased cookie sheets.

3 Bake 8 to 10 minutes or until set but not browned. Remove to wire racks; cool completely. Stack cookies in decorative muffin pan cups and pack into tins.

METRIC CONVERSION CHART

VOLUME MEASUREMENTS (dry)

1/8 teaspoon = 0.5 mL
1/4 teaspoon = 1 mL
1/2 teaspoon = 2 mL
3/4 teaspoon = 4 mL
1 teaspoon = 5 mL
1 tablespoon = 15 mL
2 tablespoons = 30 mL
1/4 cup = 60 mL
1/3 cup = 75 mL
1/2 cup = 125 mL
2/3 cup = 150 mL
3/4 cup = 175 mL
1 cup = 250 mL
2 cups = 1 pint = 500 mL
3 cups = 750 mL
4 cups = 1 quart = 1 L

VOLUME MEASUREMENTS (fluid)

1 fluid ounce (2 tablespoons) = 30 mL
4 fluid ounces (1/2 cup) = 125 mL
8 fluid ounces (1 cup) = 250 mL
12 fluid ounces (1 1/2 cups) = 375 mL
16 fluid ounces (2 cups) = 500 mL

WEIGHTS (mass)

1/2 ounce = 15 g
1 ounce = 30 g
3 ounces = 90 g
4 ounces = 120 g
8 ounces = 225 g
10 ounces = 285 g
12 ounces = 360 g
16 ounces = 1 pound = 450 g

DIMENSIONS

1/16 inch = 2 mm
1/8 inch = 3 mm
1/4 inch = 6 mm
1/2 inch = 1.5 cm
3/4 inch = 2 cm
1 inch = 2.5 cm

OVEN TEMPERATURES

250°F = 120°C
275°F = 140°C
300°F = 150°C
325°F = 160°C
350°F = 180°C
375°F = 190°C
400°F = 200°C
425°F = 220°C
450°F = 230°C

BAKING PAN SIZES

Utensil	Size in Inches/Quarts	Metric Volume	Size in Centimeters
Baking or Cake Pan (square or rectangular)	8×8×2	2 L	20×20×5
	9×9×2	2.5 L	23×23×5
	12×8×2	3 L	30×20×5
	13×9×2	3.5 L	33×23×5
Loaf Pan	8×4×3	1.5 L	20×10×7
	9×5×3	2 L	23×13×7
Round Layer Cake Pan	8×1½	1.2 L	20×4
	9×1½	1.5 L	23×4
Pie Plate	8×1¼	750 mL	20×3
	9×1¼	1 L	23×3
Baking Dish or Casserole	1 quart	1 L	—
	1½ quart	1.5 L	—
	2 quart	2 L	—